ST. AUGUSTINE'S
Afterlife

TRUE TALES OF A
PARANORMAL INVESTIGATOR

RYAN DUNN

4880 Lower Valley Road • Atglen, PA 19310

Other Schiffer Books by the Author:
Savannah's Afterlife: True Tales of a Paranormal Investigator,
978-0-7643-4769-6

Savannah's Afterlife II: More True Tales of a Paranormal Investigator,
978-0-7643-5471-7

Copyright © 2024 by Ryan Dunn
Library of Congress Control Number: 2024932156

All rights reserved. No part of this work may be reproduced or used in any form or by any means—graphic, electronic, or mechanical, including photocopying or information storage and retrieval systems—without written permission from the publisher.

The scanning, uploading, and distribution of this book or any part thereof via the Internet or any other means without the permission of the publisher is illegal and punishable by law. Please purchase only authorized editions and do not participate in or encourage the electronic piracy of copyrighted materials.

"Schiffer," "Schiffer Publishing, Ltd.," and the pen and inkwell logo are registered trademarks of Schiffer Publishing, Ltd.

Woman behind the matte glass. Blurry hand and body figure © by Joe Techapanupreeda Courtesy of www.shutterstock.com.
full moon and clouds © by Altınay Dinç Courtesy of www.unsplash.com

Cover design by Jack Chappell
Type set in Dead Secretary/Times

ISBN: 978-0-7643-6815-8
Printed in India

Published by Schiffer Publishing, Ltd.
4880 Lower Valley Road
Atglen, PA 19310
Phone: (610) 593-1777; Fax: (610) 593-2002
Email: info@schifferbooks.com
Web: www.schifferbooks.com

For our complete selection of fine books on this and related subjects, please visit our website at www.schifferbooks.com. You may also write for a free catalog.

Schiffer Publishing's titles are available at special discounts for bulk purchases for sales promotions or premiums. Special editions, including personalized covers, corporate imprints, and excerpts, can be created in large quantities for special needs. For more information, contact the publisher.

DEDICATION

*I would like to dedicate this book to the memory of my father,
David Richard Dunn.*

I miss you more and more each day.

CONTENTS

ACKNOWLEDGMENTS 06

PREFACE... 07

CHAPTER 1:   St. Augustine's Tragic Past 09

CHAPTER 2:   Dolly Dearest: The Antiques and Uniques
             Collectibles Investigation..................................... 14

CHAPTER 3:   Lily and Her Lover:
             The St. Francis Inn Investigation 20

CHAPTER 4:   The Ghost of Judge Stickney:
             The Huguenot Cemetery Investigation 25

CHAPTER 5:   Death on Display: The Casa de Sueños
             Bed-and-Breakfast Investigation........................ 30

CHAPTER 6:   Rub a Dub Dub, a Dead Man in a Tub:
             The Scarlett O'Hara's Restaurant Investigation 34

CHAPTER 7:   The Old Indian Village:
             The Tolomato Cemetery Investigation................. 39

CHAPTER 8:   The Three "Rs":
             The Oldest Wooden Schoolhouse Investigation 45

CHAPTER 9:   House of Wax:
             The Potter's Wax Museum Investigation............. 50

CHAPTER 10: A Beacon for the Spirits:
             The St. Augustine Lighthouse Investigation 56

CHAPTER 11:	If These Walls Could Talk: The Castillo de San Marcos Investigation	60
CHAPTER 12:	Ammunition for a Haunting: The Old Powder House Inn Investigation	66
CHAPTER 13:	Fallen Heroes: The St. Augustine National Cemetery Investigation	70
CHAPTER 14:	The Architect's Ghost: The Casablanca Inn Investigation	74
CHAPTER 15:	The Lady in the Window: The Prince of Wales Restaurant Investigation	78
CHAPTER 16:	The Cemetery That Time Forgot: The San Sebastian Cemetery Investigation	83
CHAPTER 17:	Palace of the Odd: The Ripley's Believe It or Not! Museum Investigation	87
CHAPTER 18:	Lavender and Mr. T: The Kenwood Inn Investigation	92
CHAPTER 19:	Levitating Objects: The Agustin Inn Investigation	96
CHAPTER 20:	The Old Well: The 44 Spanish Street Inn Investigation	100

AFTERWORD 106

BIBLIOGRAPHY 109

ACKNOWLEDGMENTS

I have a lot of people to thank who made this book possible, so I apologize in advance because this is going to be a lengthy list. If I have forgotten anyone, I am truly sorry, and I sincerely did not mean to leave you out.

Above all, I would like to thank my Lord and Savior Jesus Christ, who through Him all things are possible. Next, I would like to thank my beautiful wife, Kim Dunn. Thank you for sharing a passion for the strange and unusual with me; I am so glad we are in this together. Thank you to my two daughters, Addison and Jennifer; you inspire me every day to be a better person. Also thank you to my English bulldog, Griswold, for keeping me company while I wrote this book.

Thanks to Joni Clawges for telling me about Antiques and Uniques; that was an awesome investigation, and we caught a ton of evidence. Thank you, Denice and Larry Altman, for allowing us to investigate there, and to Dr. John de Salvo for adopting Chloe and Meredith. A huge debt of gratitude goes out to Charles Tingley and the entire staff at the St. Augustine Historical Society; I could not have done it without you. I owe a ton of thanks to Linda Lorhke and her husband, Steve, as well as the whole staff at St. Francis Inn and Casa de Sueños; we had very successful investigations at both locations. Thanks to Jasmine Staples and everyone at Scarlett O Hara's; we had a great night communicating with the ghost of George! Stephen Tighe at REAP Paranormal: it was a pleasure working with you, sir. I look forward to many more cases together. Thank you, Jake Firth and Trish Nease, for allowing us to investigate the Prince of Wales Restaurant—what a great place. Brian Funk and Emory McClune at the 44 Spanish Street Inn: you guys are two of the most gracious hosts ever, and the breakfast was wonderful. Audra Hull and Aubrey Roberts at the Agustin Inn: thank you for being so accommodating and helpful with the investigation. Pat Dobosz and everyone at the Kenwood Inn: I appreciate your hospitality and sharing your experiences with me. Thank you to Lauri Carter of the Village Paranormal; I had a blast investigating the Casablanca Inn and Prince of Wales Restaurant with you.

Guieneverre Cutlip, thank you so much for being my editor and making sure everything was in place before the manuscript went to my publisher. This book wouldn't be the same without you.

To my best friend, Mike Dixon, thanks for always being there, man. Thanks to all my brothers in Tau Kappa Epsilon Fraternity; go TKE! And last, but most definitely not least, thank you to Pete Schiffer and everyone at Schiffer Books for publishing my works and for all that you do for me as an author.

PREFACE

Before you begin reading the stories within these pages, I wanted to take just a brief moment to tell you who I am and how this book came to be. My name is Ryan Dunn, and I am a paranormal investigator, ghost tour owner, loving husband, and father to two beautiful girls and an English bulldog. My journey into the world of the paranormal began back in 2010, when my wife, Kim, and I decided to pack up and move to Savannah, Georgia, for a new start in a city that had captured our hearts. We moved into an old Victorian row house that was built in 1888—and little did we know, but the place was also haunted.

Although most people would move out if they discovered that their home was inhabited by ghosts, we have always had an interest in the paranormal. We began doing paranormal research, which led to the development of our team, the Savannah Ghost Research Society. Over the past decade, we have investigated hundreds of locations in Savannah, Georgia, and St. Augustine, Florida, as well as other locations throughout the United States. We have aired on A&E's *My Ghost Story: Caught on Camera*, SyFy Channel's *Paranormal Witness*, Travel Channel's *Most Terrifying Places* and *Haunted U.S.A.*, and *Paranormal Lockdown*, which featured Nick Groff from the *Ghost Adventures* show and Katrina Weidman from the show *Portals to Hell*, as well as numerous other programs.

In April 2013, we opened Afterlife Tours in Savannah, Georgia, which is a walking ghost tour that has 100 percent historically accurate information and features locations that we have investigated and paranormal evidence that we have collected at each stop. We do all our background research at the Historical Society to provide accurate year-by-year histories of each location that we investigate. In fall of 2018, we expanded our tour company to St. Augustine, Florida, to include locations that we have investigated there.

I first came to St. Augustine in July 2018; a colleague of mine, Joni Clawges, had told me about a haunted shop there called Antiques and Uniques. She had been investigating the shop for years and said that it was extremely haunted. The shop would be closing for good in just a few short weeks, so I contacted the owner, Denise Altman, and set up an investigation—which just so happens to be the first story in this book. As soon as I arrived in town that evening, I fell in love with the place. I knew immediately that we had to start doing more investigations here, and following years of research and numerous cases in the city, it led to the writing of this book.

This is my first book on St. Augustine's hauntings; however, I do have three books I have written on hauntings in Savannah, Georgia: *Savannah's Afterlife:*

True Tales of a Paranormal Investigator, Savannah's Afterlife II: More True Tales of a Paranormal Investigator, and *Savannah's Afterlife III: Even More True Tales of a Paranormal Investigator.* As with those books, I have taken great care to ensure that everything you are about to read is pure fact. As mentioned, all the locations have been meticulously researched at the St. Augustine Historical Society, and every place has been investigated by our team. Also, all the names of people in this book are real; nothing has been changed or omitted.

Special note: Throughout these pages, you will hear the term EVP (electronic voice phenomena) mentioned several times. An EVP is an audio recording of a ghost. We capture these by turning on an audio recorder in a haunted location. We then begin by asking questions such as "Can you tell us your name?" The majority of the time we do not hear a response on location. However, in some instances when we play the recording back, we are able to hear a spirit voice in response. Along with video and photographic evidence, EVPs are some of the most compelling findings we have been able to document in the field.

I sincerely hope that by reading this book you fall in love with the city of St. Augustine as I did. With its rich history, lush palm trees, and historic homes, the place is paradise. Considering that it is the oldest city in the United States, there is no wonder that the town is filled with ghosts. The stories you are about to read are the real accounts of some of the most haunted places in the city. I will dispel the myths that have been told about these places over the years, and you will discover what truly happened. As they say, truth is stranger than fiction.

CHAPTER 1

ST. AUGUSTINE'S TRAGIC PAST

The Old City Gates were constructed from coquina and date back to the year 1808.

Most historians attribute the discovery of Florida to Juan Ponce de León, who was a Spanish explorer and conquistador as well as the first governor of Puerto Rico. In spring 1513, he led an expedition that settled along the eastern coast of Florida. They arrived on land during the Easter season, and he claimed the land for Spain. He named the newly discovered land La Florida in reverence to the holiday, which in Spain is known as Pascua Florida. Although popular belief is that he was searching for the famed Fountain of Youth, there is no evidence to suggest that this was true. Correspondence between him and King

Ferdinand never mentioned this fictional fountain. Some sources do mention, however, that the local Taíno Indians believed that there was a magic fountain and healing river in an area north of Cuba.

During the next few decades, several expeditions were launched to explore and colonize Florida, but no gold and riches were found, much to the bitter disappointment of the Spanish. In 1562, a group of French Protestants known as the Huguenots, under the guidance of explorer and navigator Jean Ribault, established a settlement on Parris Island, South Carolina, called Charlesfort. Two years later, three ships filled with French Huguenots, under explorer Rene Goulaine de Laudonniere, set sail and established a fort along the St. John's River near what is now Jacksonville. They named their new settlement Fort Caroline.

In order to protect his claim on Florida for the Spanish Crown, King Phillip II of Spain decided to establish a permanent settlement there along the coast. He selected Pedro Menéndez de Avilés to lead the expedition. Menéndez held the highest naval rank in Spain: that of captain general of the armada. While preparations for the long voyage were underway, the king received news of Laudonniere's expedition and was concerned that the French were jeopardizing his hold on the land of Florida. The fact that he was a devout Catholic stoked his anger even further that these Protestant Huguenots were settling on his land. He then instructed Menéndez to destroy the French settlement at Fort Caroline once he arrived in the New World.

Menéndez and the colonists set sail for Florida in May 1565. On August 28, 1565, land was spotted. This just so happened to be the date of the Feast of St. Augustine, which resulted in the colony's name. A couple of weeks later, on September 10, Jean Ribault sailed to St. Augustine with troops to attack the new colony. A storm carried his ship far south of the city, where it wrecked along the eastern coast. At around the same time, Pedro Menéndez, along with his soldiers, marched to Fort Caroline, which they overtook rather easily, since most of the French were headed to attack St. Augustine. He killed all the men, hanging their bodies from the trees with the inscription "Hanged not as Frenchmen but as heretics." Only the women and children were spared and shipped to Havana, Cuba.

He then marched to the beach just a few miles outside St. Augustine, where he and his soldiers captured 127 Huguenots. Through a translator, Menéndez told the French how he had just conquered Fort Caroline and that he suggested they surrender. It has been said that he offered to spare their lives, but there is no record to suggest such. Francisco Mendoza, who was Menéndez's priest, suggested that they spare the lives of those who would confess and turn to Catholicism. The majority refused and were slaughtered on the spot. Out of the 127 men, only 16 were spared.

On October 12, 1565, more Huguenots, among them Jean Ribault, arrived on the inlet and surrendered to Menéndez and his men. This time 134 men were slaughtered, wiping out the remainder of the French Huguenots in Florida. It was said that the bay ran red with blood from all the dead bodies, and from then on it has been called Matanzas Bay, which means "massacres" or "slaughters" in Spanish. This is how Menéndez earned himself the nickname "the Butcher of Avilés."

A PIRATE ATTACK

In the summer 1586, English privateer and sea captain Sir Francis Drake attacked St. Augustine. This was just six years after he had become the first Englishman to circumnavigate the entire globe. Often described as a pirate because of his tendency to raid Spanish ships and ports, Drake arrived with twenty-three ships and nearly two thousand men. They attacked with cannon fire from nearby Anastasia Island. The following day, they stormed into the city and burned it to the ground, leaving nothing but destruction in their wake. Drake then returned to England.

THE SPREAD OF DISEASE

In 1649, St. Augustine was hit with its first yellow fever epidemic, which was believed to have been brought over by water casks on ships that had sailed into the city. This was followed by a smallpox outbreak in 1655, and then measles in 1659. In just a decade the city saw three major outbreaks of disease.

A SECOND PIRATE ATTACK

On the night of May 28, 1668, Jamaican pirate Captain Robert Searle and his crew snuck into the harbor of a sleeping city. They attacked St. Augustine by surprise, ransacking houses and pillaging buildings, leaving sixty citizens dead in the streets. They were in search of silver that was held in the royal treasury. They returned to Jamaica, where Searle was arrested in Port Royal, only to be released a few months later. He then went on to serve as a lieutenant under Sir Henry Morgan's sack of Panama City.

A CITY UNDER SIEGE (AGAIN!)

On November 10, 1702, during Queen Anne's War, Carolina governor and Englishman James Moore arrived in St. Augustine with his forces and laid siege to the city. Governor Zuniga y Zerda, who at the time was the Spanish governor of Florida, declared that the citizens of St. Augustine take shelter in the Castillo de San Marcos during the bombardment. Nearly 1,500 citizens, along with hundreds of soldiers, were walled up inside the fort's massive walls. Moore and his troops continued their attack on the fort with cannon fire, which had little effect on its coquina walls.

By Christmas Eve, supply ships arrived in St. Augustine from Charles Towne to add support to Moore's forces. Two days later, four men-of-war appeared in the harbor as reinforcements for the Spanish. Moore and his soldiers were forced to give up the attack and retreat, ending the nearly two-month attack on the Castillo de San Marcos. Although he wasn't able to conquer the fort and take the city, much of the town was left in ruins by the bombardment.

THE SIEGE OF 1740

In May 1740, St. Augustine was attacked for a fourth time. General James Oglethorpe, the founder of the Georgia colony, had arrived just off the coast of the city with seven ships. Once again, the citizens of the town walled themselves up within the walls of the Castillo de San Marcos. For the next twenty-seven days, the English attacked the fort. After nearly a month, they were running low on supplies, and it seemed that the Castillo was impenetrable. Oglethorpe and his men retreated, much to his chagrin.

MORE DISEASE

In 1821, St. Augustine suffered its worst yellow fever epidemic. Ships arriving from Havana, Cuba, brought the disease into the city. Throughout the following months, one-third of the population perished from the fever, with dozens of people dying daily. As the death toll mounted, local priests struggled to keep up with the high number of funerals, and doctors worked around the clock to treat their dying patients. As the fall brought cooler weather, the mosquito population began to die off, which slowed the number of yellow fever cases.

A NEW ERA

In the late 1800s, magnate Henry Flagler, who was a partner and cofounder in Standard Oil with John D. Rockefeller, took a keen interest in the city of St. Augustine. While visiting the town on a honeymoon with his second wife, Ida, he decided that it would be an excellent vacation spot for America's upper class. He returned in 1885 and began construction on a boutique hotel. The Ponce de Leon Hotel opened its doors in 1888 to the nation's elite, complete with 540 luxurious rooms and featuring Tiffany-stained glass in the dining room. Among the famous guests who stayed there were Theodore Roosevelt, Babe Ruth, Robert Frost, Somerset Maugham, Ernest Hemingway, Mark Twain, and Zora Neal Thurston, just to name a few. In 1888, Flagler built a second hotel, the Alcazar, directly across the street from the Ponce. In addition to his contributions to St. Augustine's hotels, Flagler also developed the Florida East Coast Railway, which by 1912 extended all the way to Key West. To this day, he is given credit for bringing tourism to St. Augustine and the rest of coastal Florida.

The Bridge of Lions connects downtown St. Augustine to nearby Anastasia Island across Matanzas Bay. The pair of lions that guard the bridge are copies of the marble Medici lions that are in Rome, Italy. *Photo by Kim Dunn*

    The next century saw extensive renovation in the historic homes and buildings throughout the city. As tourism grew, so did the demand for upkeep on these centuries-old structures. Today, it is one of the most popular tourist destinations in the state of Florida. Founded in 1565, it is the oldest continuously inhabited European settlement in the United States, and the oldest city in the nation. Although Jamestown is the oldest English settlement in the country, dating back to the year 1607, St. Augustine is several years older. With its tragic past as well as its age, St. Augustine has earned its place among America's most haunted cities.

The Antiques and Uniques Collectibles Investigation

Antiques and Uniques houses an assortment of haunted objects for sale.

I first heard about the hauntings at Antiques and Uniques Collectibles, located at Seven Aviles Street, from my colleague, good friend, and fellow investigator Joni Clawges. We met over the years when she came to Savannah to investigate, and she would always take our tour. At the time, we were looking to expand our ghost tour company into St. Augustine, and Joni said that we needed to investigate Antiques and Uniques.

The owners, Larry and Denice Altman, were very open to letting paranormal teams investigate the building, and she herself had investigated there multiple times. According to Joni, the place was extremely active. A lot of the activity took place in the far backroom of the shop. On a previous investigation, Joni was in that room and had just sat down on the floor to conduct an EVP session. As soon as she sat down, her audio recorder caught an EVP of a female entity that said, "Disgraceful. Get off the floor." In colonial times, it was unheard of for a "lady" to sit on the floor, and it wouldn't have been considered "proper." This spirit was not happy that a female had decided to sit on the floor. In today's times, this would not matter one bit, but for all we know, this spirit could've died more than two hundred or three hundred years ago.

THE OLD JAIL

The building itself had quite an interesting history. This two-story structure was built in the year 1888 as the city jail. During this time, it was used to house petty criminals—primarily as a holding tank for drunk and disorderly citizens. All the more serious criminals were kept in the county lockup just outside town. Although it was originally built as a one-story stone jail, the second story was later added in 1899.

By 1904 the building was converted into office spaces, and then by 1925 a man named Brandon Hall opened a sporting-goods store there. The store continued to operate until the late 1960s, when it was converted into the Aviles Ice Cream Parlor, operated by Henry Whetstone and his wife, Esther. The Whetstones were also the founders of Whetstone Chocolates, which has been an iconic St. Augustine landmark since its founding in 1967. Throughout the mid-1970s and up until the year 2002, the building served as a gift and souvenir shop, craft store, and card store. It was then vacant for a few years, until 2006, when Larry and Denice Altman opened Antiques and Uniques Collectibles there.

According to Denice, the building is haunted by multiple entities. She has felt the presence of a young girl in the store on numerous occasions. One of the more ominous spirits, however, is the presence of a man. The apparition of a tall dark figure in a long coat with tails appears in the backrooms on many occasions, pacing back and forth. Denice has security cameras set up throughout the store, and on more than one occasion, they have picked up this entity walking around in the building.

CHLOE AND MEREDITH

Although many of the spirits here seem attached to the location, some of the paranormal encounters in the place may be attributed to haunted objects that Denice has brought into the shop throughout the years. Some of these items can possibly contain spiritual attachments. The famous ghost-hunting duo Ed and

Chloe and Meredith both like to move on their own.

Lorraine Warren, from which the Conjuring movies were based, made an entire career of dealing with haunted objects, as well as demonic cases. In fact, many of their case files are necessary reading for anyone who first joins our paranormal research team, the Savannah Ghost Research Society.

Two such objects that cause a lot of activity in the shop are a pair of dolls that Denice purchased a few years back at an estate sale in Mississippi. They are named Chloe and Meredith. Ever since she bought the dolls, the two began to cause activity in the shop. Chloe has been known to turn her head back and forth on her own, and Meredith likes to change positions and roll her eyes at Denice. About a year ago, a man came into the shop and purchased Meredith for his young wife. The very next day, the man returned to the shop, and he was very distraught.

"Please take this doll back; I don't want it anymore," he said to the Altmans.

Larry then informed the man that they do not accept refunds.

"I don't care about the money," said the man. "I just want you to take it back. My wife saw it move on its own."

After that incident, the dolls have remained in the store ever since. Recently, however, Denice donated the dolls to Dr. John DeSalvo, who is a biophysicist, professor, and well-known researcher in the paranormal field. He is also a collector of historical religious artifacts and haunted objects. John has reported capturing numerous EVPs and other activity from the dolls since he received them.

In October 2012, Antiques and Uniques Collectibles aired on A&E's hit television show My Ghost Story: Caught on Camera (season 5, episode 5, titled "Leave Those Kids Alone"). During the episode, a video anomaly was captured that caused a flashlight to turn on by itself. A few years later, in early October 2016, when Hurricane Matthew came through, it flooded much of the city. The wine shop that sits on Charlotte Street, the street located just behind this building, had to replace their floor due to water damage. Archeologists were invited to look into the earth underneath the floor, and when they did, they made a gruesome discovery.

HIDDEN BURIALS

The remains of seven corpses, including three children, were discovered beneath the ground. The bodies dated back to the mid- to late 1500s. In addition, part of a thatch roof was discovered that is believed to be part of the Church of Nuestra Señora de la Remedios, the parish church that was built in St. Augustine soon after the colony was established. The bodies were believed to be from burials beneath the church floor. The church had been destroyed during Sir Francis Drake's raid on the city in 1586. Unfortunately, in August 2018 the owner of the building decided to put it up for sale, and he wouldn't allow the Altmans to renew their lease. The building remains vacant along Aviles Street and may remain so for quite some time.

THE INVESTIGATION

I had been excited to start investigating locations in St. Augustine for quite a while, and in early June 2018, I received a call from Joni Clawges telling me that Antiques and Uniques Collectibles would be closing its doors for good within the following two months. I knew that if I was ever going to investigate there, I had better do it quickly. I called Denice, and we set a date for a few weeks later, on July 1.

I arrived that night, just after closing with two other investigators. Within the first five minutes of entering the building, I suddenly became very sick to my stomach. As soon as I walked outside, the strange feeling abated. I stayed outside for about ten minutes, and when I reentered the store, I began to feel sick again. There was something about the place that seemed to be physically affecting me. Regardless of how I was feeling, I had to push through it.

After all our equipment was set up, we immediately headed to the back office to conduct an EVP session. Within the first few minutes, one of our audio recorders picked up an EVP that said, "Kill them." It then became apparent that at least one of the entities in the building was not happy with our presence there. A few minutes later, a static recorder that had been left near the front of the store picked up another EVP. This one was of a deep male voice that said, "Professionals." I wonder if it was perhaps referring to there being investigators in the building.

A little later into the night, we decided to do a few EVP sessions with the haunted dolls, Chloe and Meredith. Within the first few minutes, we caught a very clear EVP that seemed to be in a young female voice that said, "We hate the girl too, but I'm watching him." This was interesting, because one of the three investigators there that night was female.

At around the same time, I was scanning the area with the structured light sensor (SLS) camera when a strange incident happened. The SLS camera is a multifaceted scanning camera that reads the environment by using Kinect sensors that send information back to the camera. They will detect temperature, distance, audio, and light levels. These will sometimes pick up apparitions that will appear on the camera as small stick figures. One of our team members who was sitting on the floor at that time reported feeling a strange sensation on his leg. At about that same time, the SLS camera picked up a small figure that appeared to be sitting on his lap. The figure was the size of a small child. It stayed in the same area for just a few moments, and then it disappeared entirely. At the time it disappeared, the investigator reported that the sensation went away immediately.

Although Antiques and Uniques Collectibles closed in August 2018, Larry and Denice Altman continue to search for a new location for their store. They make regular appearances on podcasts and radio shows in which they talk about the experiences they encountered while in the old store. The building itself remains vacant, and it is the first stop on our St. Augustine ghost tour.

Perhaps, one day, someone new will acquire the place, but until then, all the energy there will continue to build and fester as it lies in wait for its future occupants. Note: the building is now private property, and trepassing is not allowed.

LILY AND HER LOVER:

The St. Francis Inn Investigation

The St. Francis Inn is one of the most well-known haunted inns in the city.

At the corner of St. George and St. Francis Streets sits the Spanish colonial building that is now known as the St. Francis Inn. This beautiful building, also known locally as the Garcia-Dummett House, was constructed in the year 1791 on a king's grant for Sergeant Gaspar Garcia of the Third Battalion of the Infantry Regiment of Cuba, which was stationed in St. Augustine. Garcia was the quartermaster of the Spanish troops in town.

Only four years after the home was built, in 1795, Garcia sold the home to Rafael Saavedra de Espinoza, who then sold the home two months later to Mateo Guadarrama, who was a businessman and speculator in real estate. Throughout the next forty-three years, the home changed hands numerous times, until 1838, when it was sold to a wealthy sugar planter from Barbados named Colonel Thomas Henry Dummett.

Dummett was of English descent and had served in the British marines. He had been forced to flee Barbados when there was an uprising of his enslaved workers. He barely escaped alive by hiding in a sugar cask that had been placed aboard a ship by his enslaved men, on which he then sailed to America in safety. After a short while in Connecticut, he moved with his family to Florida in search of a much-warmer climate. After arriving in Florida, he established a 3,500-acre sugar plantation just outside New Smyrna, Florida. After this plantation was later destroyed by natives during the Second Seminole War, the Dummett family moved back to St. Augustine in 1838.

Unfortunately, Colonel Dummett passed away within the first year of owning the home, but the property remained in the Dummett family for the next fifty years. In 1840, his daughter, Elizabeth, married William J. Hardee, a native of Georgia and a graduate of West Point. Hardee's book *Rifle and Light Infantry Tactics,* published in 1855, was adopted as a textbook for the US Army. During the Civil War, he served in the Confederacy as a lieutenant general in battles at Shiloh, at Missionary Ridge, and in Atlanta. After Elizabeth's death, the home was given to her sister, Anna Dummett, who lived out the rest of her life there.

An article in the local newspaper in 1899 stated, "Miss Anna Dummett, who has resided in this city more than sixty years, died Thursday morning about 5:30 o'clock. She had a fall Wednesday morning and did not rally. Miss Dummett was born in Barbados eighty-two years ago, and was the daughter of a sugar planter who moved to Florida when she was eighteen years of age, and secured the house at the corner of St. George and St. Francis Streets, where she died." A few years later, in 1904, the building was transformed into the Teahan Hotel, which was operated by W. M. Teahan, and then, by 1919, it was converted into the Amity Apartments.

FAMOUS AUTHORS

In the 1930s, the home became the Graham House and was used as rental cottages. During that period, it became home to several resident authors. The first of these was Van Wyck Brooks, who came to stay in St. Augustine in 1933 to recover from a breakdown that left him "like a living dead man." Brooks was the author of *The Wine of the Puritans* and *The Malady of the Ideal*, as well as other notable works. He was also famous for coining the terms "lowbrow" and "highbrow."

A year later, in 1934, author Edith Pope lived at the Graham House for a short time. Pope was the author of *Black Lagoon and Other Verses*, *Not Magnolia*, and *Old Lady Asteroy*, as well as other works.

Once again, in 1937, the Graham House played host to yet another literary resident. In that year, author Gladys Hasty Carroll, well known for her work *As the Earth Turns*, visited St. Augustine and stayed at the Graham House for about two weeks.

Guests at the St. Francis Inn have reported a female presence in what is known as Lily's Room.

By 1950, Ralph Moody purchased the home and reopened the place as the St. Francis Inn. Up until the present, it has continued to operate as the St. Francis Inn, although it has changed ownership many times over the years. In 1985, the current owners, Joe and Margaret Finnegan, purchased the place. Ever since, they have continued to operate one of the most successful bed-and-breakfasts in St. Augustine.

LILY

The most well-known ghost story about the St. Francis Inn concerns a ghost named Lily. Lily was a young enslaved girl who was owned by the home's previous owner, Colonel William Hardee. As the story goes, one of the colonel's nephews became smitten with Lily, and the two developed a secret affair. It wasn't long before the two fell in love. After some time, the nephew decided that he wanted to marry Lily, something the colonel vehemently opposed. After being denied the privilege of marrying his love, the nephew committed suicide by hanging himself from the rafters in the attic of the home. One version of the story states that after discovering the body of her young lover, Lily then killed herself as well. Another version suggests that she lived out the rest of her life in the home, crying nonstop for her ill-fated love.

Even though the story of Lily and her lover is probably the most famous tale surrounding the old inn, there is no record to suggest that it happened. We were able to find records of all the enslaved people owned by Colonel Hardee, and he never owned an enslaved girl named Lily. In addition, none of his nephews died by suicide or anything of the sort. Perhaps the illustrious tale was created because there is indeed the presence of a female spirit that haunts the building. Sometimes, to give name to a presence, employees and various owners have been known to concoct a tragic backstory to account for their ghosts when no other ready explanation is available. Maybe this tragic tale had been created by a previous owner here to account for this female entity.

Much of the paranormal activity that occurs in the inn centers on the apparition of a young girl in a white dress that roams the halls, particularly on the third floor. Over the years, she has come to be known as Lily, earning her name from the main character in the famous story that surrounds the inn. Numerous guests staying there have seen her walking in the halls only to disappear moments later. Others have reported unexplainable icy touches by unseen hands, as well as extreme cold spots and uneasy feelings, particularly in "Lily's Room," as well as in the hallways.

The most haunted room in the inn is on the third floor, which used to be the attic, and it is aptly named "Lily's Room." Female guests staying in the room have found the contents of their purses emptied on the floor, and all their belongings scattered across the room. On one occasion, a man woke up the next morning underneath the bed. He couldn't fathom how he had gotten there, since he had fallen asleep in the bed the night before. He was stuck underneath the bed and had to call for help to get out.

One night a few years ago, a newlywed couple was staying in Lily's Room. The bride was woken up in the middle of the night by a deep passionate kiss. She then opened her eyes, only to find her husband lying fast asleep beside her. She immediately woke him, and he assured her that it had not been him who had kissed her only a few moments before. Aside from the ghost of Lily, many have reported the apparition of a young man in their room. He has been seen by many guests, as well as employees, walking near the stairway.

One of my good friends Michael Teleoglou had a strange experience at the inn. He was staying in Lily's Room, and one afternoon while returning to the room he noticed that his key was missing. He went downstairs and told the front desk, and their reaction was, "Oh here we go again!" He asked them further, and they said that the ghost of Lily likes to take the room keys from guests that she likes.

With all the amazing stories about the hauntings there, it is no wonder that this was the first haunted inn that I investigated in St. Augustine. When I arrived one hot afternoon in late July 2018 for the case, I was greeted by Linda Lohrke, who was more than happy to tell me about all the haunted activity that occurred there. Her husband, Steve Lohrke, who is also mentioned later in this book, was the concierge at their sister property, the Casa de Sueños Bed and Breakfast, which is also known to be haunted. In fact, it was because of her suggestion that I set up an investigation there a few weeks later. I cannot thank the Lohrkes enough for their assistance and time, which made these two investigations possible.

THE INVESTIGATION

As soon as I arrived, I was led up to Lily's Room, which would be my accommodation for the night. As soon as I entered the room, I could feel a very heavy presence all around me. There was nothing that felt threatening, but there was something there all the same. Perhaps this would account for the fact that all the paranormal evidence captured during the investigation happened to be in this room. Although many hours were spent using various pieces of equipment, I managed to capture only two EVPs, both of which were in this room, and both were caught within a two-to-three-minute time frame.

At 8:49 p.m., while I was conducting an EVP session in Lily's Room, I asked, "Can you tell me why you want me to get out?" Just a few minutes earlier, I thought that I had caught an EVP that said, "Get out," which upon further review was just static; hence my reason for the question. A few seconds later, my audio recorder picked up an EVP of a deep male voice that replied, "I was just kidding." Less than two minutes later, another EVP was captured in the same voice that said, "Leave." I couldn't tell for sure, but it seemed that this entity was toying with me. Throughout the rest of the investigation, no more evidence was captured, but both of these EVPs were Class A and very clear.

After my investigation and overnight stay there, I have no doubt that the St. Francis Inn is haunted. Judging from the evidence caught during the investigation, as well as the reports from the staff regarding their paranormal encounters, there is at least one male and one female presence that haunts the building, perhaps even more. The accommodations there are second to none, and the breakfast I had the next morning was amazing. Linda and the staff at the inn are wonderful, and this is one of the nicest stays you will find in St. Augustine. They also have a beautiful courtyard and pool, and there are bicycles available to all their guests for a scenic ride throughout this beautiful historic city.

CHAPTER 4

THE GHOST OF JUDGE STICKNEY:
The Huguenot Cemetery Investigation

The Huguenot Cemetery, contrary to its name, isn't believed to contain any burials of members of the Huguenots.

In 1821, at the onset of one of St. Augustine's major yellow fever epidemics, the Huguenot Cemetery was opened for Protestant burials. Over the years, the graveyard has been known as "the Burying Ground," "the Public Burying Ground," "the Protestant Ground," "the Old Protestant Graveyard," and "City Gate Cemetery." It was later named "Huguenot Cemetery," which is interesting because, contrary to its name, there are no Huguenots buried there. It was believed that the yellow fever came from ships that arrived in St. Augustine from Havana, Cuba. Three to four of these vessels arrived in the city with the majority of the crew dead from the disease. One ship came with the entire crew and captain dead on board, with only one sailor and a cook still alive. They died from yellow fever a few days after their arrival. It was believed that mosquitoes in the ship's water barrels were carrying the disease. These sailors had unknowingly brought yellow fever to St. Augustine.

One of the most famous stories about the cemetery is that there is a mass grave of yellow fever victims within the cemetery. Although there are no records either to prove or disprove that theory, with the number of deaths occurring at that time, this was likely true. Although there are ninety-four existing memorials in the cemetery, according to records there are many more unmarked graves within the burial ground.

DEATH IS ALL AROUND

In October 1821, as the disease was running rampant, a man named Reverend Andrew Fowler from Charleston, South Carolina, arrived in St. Augustine with the hopes of establishing a new church in the city. With yellow fever spreading throughout the town, the reverend found himself, instead, tending to the city's sick and dying. During his two-month stay in St. Augustine, the reverend performed ninety-five funerals. One soldier stationed there wrote home that people in the city were "dying thirteen to fourteen a day from the disease, including soldiers." According to a US Army unit stationed in St. Augustine at the time, one-third of the population of St. Augustine died of yellow fever in 1821. This is the same proportion of death reported in Havana, Cuba, during its first yellow fever epidemic in 1649.

There were numerous reports of people being buried alive in Huguenot Cemetery, especially during the height of the town's 1821 yellow fever epidemic. After the victim had bled from the mouth, nose, eyes, and ears, and the internal organs had shut down and liquefied into a thick black goo, the victim's skin would turn a jaundiced-yellow color; hence the name. Another nickname for the disease was black vomit, because as your internal organs began to putrefy, you would begin to throw them up. The disease would often lead to a state of paralysis, and oftentimes, people were pronounced dead when in fact they were still alive. This unfortunately often led to premature burials.

The cemetery served as a Protestant burial ground throughout the majority of the 1800s.

Burial plots at the Huguenot Cemetery were originally four dollars a plot. While now that doesn't seem like much, back then for St. Augustine's poor and destitute that was a lot of money. To save money, many poor families would purchase one plot, and after someone new died, they would dig the plot back up and put new bodies in with the old corpses in the casket. In some cases, upon opening the casket they found scratch marks on the inside of the lid, indicating that those folks had indeed been buried alive.

JUDGE STICKNEY

In early November 1882, telegrams began arriving in St. Augustine from Washington, DC, concerning the health of the US attorney for the Northern District of Florida. The attorney, former judge John B. Stickney, who had come to St. Augustine following the Civil War, had gone to Washington on business despite being sick with dengue fever. Dengue fever is a mosquito-borne tropical disease caused by the dengue virus. Symptoms typically begin anywhere from three to fourteen days after infection. This may include a high fever, a headache, vomiting, muscle and joint pains, and a skin rash. Recovery generally takes two to seven days, but in some cases the disease can advance and result in death. Within a week, a train was bringing the judge's dead body back home. The remains were met by a delegation from the Duval County Bar, who accompanied the judge's body back to St. Augustine. According to the notice in the Jacksonville, Florida, newspaper, "Judge Stickney was interred in the Protestant Cemetery in St. Augustine."

On July 10, 1884, both the Tolomato Cemetery and the Huguenot Cemetery were closed to new burials. It was believed in those times that decaying matter, along with the moisture in low-lying areas, was giving off poisonous fumes that caused illness. The idea of burying people within city limits was thought to spread disease. Author Mark Twain (Samuel Clemens), in his work *Life of Mississippi*, supported this argument and advised against continuing to bury the dead in the ground. He favored the process of cremation instead of burial.

RETURNING HOME

In 1903, twenty-one years after Judge John B. Stickney's burial, his children, who were living in Washington, DC, at the time, decided they wanted his body moved to be buried alongside his family. The arrangements were made for an exhumation, and a professional gravedigger was hired. During the opening of the grave, a group of curious people started to assemble, interested in seeing a corpse in a state of decomposition. At that same time, two drunk men were strolling down the street and wanted to see the body. When the gravedigger turned around and looked, the judge's lower jawbone was missing! One of the men had stolen it because it contained some of the judge's gold teeth. The men took off down the street with their prize and were never seen again. The local newspaper described the incident as "an outrage." The judge has been seen haunting the cemetery ever since, wearing a long black coat and a tall dark hat, still looking at the ground for his missing teeth. He is also known to chase away anyone who sneaks into the cemetery at night. Supposedly he wants to be sure that no one else's grave is disturbed after what happened to his corpse.

The grave of Judge Stickney still sits in the cemetery, although his body was reinterred in Virginia many years ago.

On May 7, 2011, the Huguenot Cemetery aired on season 2, episode 6, of My Ghost Story: Caught on Camera on the A&E Biography Channel. The episode was titled "Smiling Ghost."

THE INVESTIGATION

In the summer of 2018, we finally had the chance to investigate the Huguenot Cemetery. While strolling through the old grounds, I couldn't help but wonder how many unmarked graves were beneath my feet. When I am in a cemetery I always try to walk between the rows and around the graves to respect the dead and not walk over them. In this case, however, I wasn't sure if it was possible to do this, since there are quite possibly many burials with no markers.

Although there was an overwhelming sense of sadness here, I managed to capture only a few EVPs during the investigation. The most chilling of these occurred after I asked, "Why are you still here? What keeps you here in this cemetery?" Right afterward, a gravelly deep male voice responded with "I'm sick." I couldn't help but feel that this was the spirit of one of the many people buried there who had died during the yellow fever epidemic of 1821. After a while, everything seemed to be quiet, and I hadn't been getting any responses or activity, so I asked, "Why will you not talk to me?" An EVP was then caught that replied with "I don't really remember." This entity seemed confused as to what I was asking, and perhaps was the spirit of a lost soul wandering there.

I was thrilled to be able to walk away from this investigation with some amazing audio evidence. Many people still report seeing the ghost of Judge Stickney wandering throughout the cemetery late at night, still searching for his jawbone and gold teeth. Unfortunately to protect its historic markers the cemetery is open to the public only on the third Saturday of every month from 11:00 a.m. until 3:00 p.m. Just don't try to sneak in at night, or you very well may encounter the ghost of the old judge.

The Huguenot Cemetery first opened to burials in the year 1821, following a major yellow fever epidemic in the city.

DEATH ON DISPLAY:
The Casa de Sueños Bed-and-Breakfast Investigation

Casa de Sueños (House of Dreams) was formerly the Garcia Funeral Home.

If you were to take a ghost tour in St. Augustine, it would be surprising if the guide didn't stop by the Casa de Sueños Bed and Breakfast. Translated in English, it means the "House of Dreams," but considering its dark past, at times it can be anything but its title. This two-story Mediterranean Revival home was erected sometime between the years 1904 and 1910. Prior to this structure being built, this area used to contain vast orange groves. This home was built for a man named George A. Colee. The Colee family had been in the carriage and livery business ever since Louis A. Colee established the St. Augustine Transfer Company in the 1880s. By the year 1914, George A. Colee was dead, and his widow, Virginia Colee, was listed as the sole occupant of the home. Throughout the 1930s and 1940s, various other widows lived in the home, and in the year 1955 the house was converted into the Garcia Funeral Home, owned by Phillip Garcia.

CORPSES ON DISPLAY

Supposedly, Mr. Garcia would place real embalmed corpses lying in open caskets that he propped up in the large front windows of the funeral home for advertisement. The idea was that he could showcase how great his embalming techniques were and that the corpses wouldn't decompose from exposure. This tale has been told on many ghost tours throughout the years. The fact is that the funeral home operated there from 1955 until 1975, and there is no way that the city or the family of the deceased would have allowed this to happen. In addition, we were able to find an old photo of the funeral home in the newspaper, and there weren't any front windows in the building during the time that the funeral home was there. That area was simply a front porch.

By 1972, Mr. Garcia's funeral director, William McGrath Jr., took over ownership of the business and renamed it the McGrath Funeral Home. In the late 1970s and early 1980s, it was listed as being owned by the St. Johns County Association for Retarded Citizens. In 1995, the home was converted into the Casa de Sueños Bed and Breakfast, which it continues to operate as today.

Prior to our investigation in mid-August 2018, I had the opportunity to sit down with the innkeeper, Steve Lohrke, who had been working there for the past nine years. During his tenure, he has had some strange encounters, and he is convinced the place is haunted. One of the more disturbing incidents happened about nine years ago, when he was first hired. Not long after starting the job, Steve began assisting the inn's new owner in converting two of the rooms into extra bedrooms. During this brief renovation period, the inn remained closed. Steve would stay and work very late hours while renovating the rooms, sometimes until even three or four o'clock in the morning. One evening, around 1:30 a.m., he was working in the inn late by himself. He had the music playing on random through the inn's old five-disc-changer CD player to keep him company. As he walked into what is now the "Nieves Room" to grab some more supplies, the atmosphere suddenly changed. The room was freezing cold as soon as he entered, and there was a very heavy, uneasy feeling present. Steve quickly grabbed his tools and went back into the room he had been working in. All of a sudden, the song that was playing on the CD player stopped midsong, and the disc changed. A few moments later, "If You Leave Me Now" by Chicago started playing. The CD then began skipping, and it was repeatedly skipping on the word "leave." "Leave . . . "Leave" . . . "Leave" . . . and it wouldn't stop. A little unnerved by the incident, Steve turned the CD player off.

Later into the night, as things became more and more quiet, he decided to turn some music back on. He went to the CD player, selected a song, and then went back to work. A few minutes later, before the song was even finished, it changed back to the Chicago song again and started skipping on "Leave" . . . "Leave" . . . "Leave" again. Steve quickly finished his work there and left for the night. Since that incident, he has tried on several occasions to play that same song again to see what would happen, but that particular track hasn't skipped. Other guests staying in the Nieves Room have reported the sensation of being touched on the shoulder by an unseen presence, only to turn around and there be no one there.

TROUBLE IN THE KITCHEN

In addition to the Nieves Room, a lot of strange activity has been reported in the kitchen. Just a few days prior to this interview, while Steve was in the kitchen, a knife fell off the magnetic strip that held the cutlery, and cut his hand. The way that the knife fell and hit him, it wasn't a natural trajectory, and it seemed propelled by some unseen force. Also in the kitchen, on occasion, pots and pans on the stove that are full of water that is about to boil slide off by themselves.

A few months before this, Steve heard a very loud explosion and couldn't find the source of the loud noise. He searched and searched, but everything seemed in order. The following day, Steve went to get an insulated coffeepot. When he opened the pot, the glass inside was completely shattered. He said that he had never witnessed anything like that before, and he thinks that this may have been the source of the loud explosion he had heard the day prior.

In addition, one Sunday night, Steve was in the inn by himself while all the guests were out. He was sitting down and eating a slice of pizza when he distinctly heard his name called out in a female voice from behind him. The voice said, "Steven." Thinking that maybe his wife had come to see him at work, he quickly turned around, but no one was there.

THE INVESTIGATION

After sitting down with Steve that evening, I couldn't wait to begin setting up my equipment and get the investigation underway. Over the past nine and a half years investigating the paranormal, I have come to realize that sometimes it's not the quantity of evidence you capture, but the quality. Throughout the entire investigation, I managed to capture only three EVPs, but what was said on each of these audio recordings sent shivers down my spine. Also, all three of these were captured in the Nieves Room.

The first of these was caught after I asked, "Would you like me to leave?" An EVP was then picked up on the recorder that replied with "Yeah." A little while later, I asked, "Do you like the fact that this place is named House of Dreams?" An EVP was then caught that replied, "No." The last EVP, however, was the most chilling. I then asked, "If you would like me to stay, then tell me to stay. If you would like me to leave, then tell me to leave." A terrifying EVP was then caught that growled, "Leave." Whoever this entity was, it did not sound friendly at all. This was amazing, because Steve had experienced something trying to tell him to leave while in the Nieves Room over nine years before. It is no wonder that this was the room with all the activity.

Although there wasn't a tremendous amount of evidence captured during the investigation of the Casa de Sueños Bed and Breakfast, what was captured was absolutely amazing. I can't thank Steve Lorhke and the staff there enough for their gracious hospitality and for allowing me access to such an amazing historic property. If you are looking for a haunted place to stay while visiting St. Augustine, what could be better than a building that was once used as a funeral home? They offer complimentary sherry for your room, which may come in handy if you should need a quick nip after a ghostly encounter while staying in the building.

CHAPTER 6

RUB A DUB DUB, A DEAD MAN IN A TUB:

The Scarlett O'Hara's Restaurant Investigation

Scarlett O'Hara's is home to the ghost of George Colee, as well as several other spirits.

A town known for its vibrant nightlife, St. Augustine has a plethora of late-night restaurants and bars. Although there are many places to choose from, one of the most interesting places you will find is Scarlett O'Hara's Restaurant. Nestled along the corners of Cordova and Hypolita Streets, they have been in operation in downtown St. Augustine for the past forty years. The home in which the restaurant sits was built in 1879 for a man named George Colee. Prior to the construction of the home, George had fought in the Seminole Wars. During a battle with the Indians in 1835, George lost one of his eyes, which earned him the nickname One-Eyed George. After the war, George received 80 acres of land that had been given to him by President Franklin Pierce in an act to give "bounty lands to soldiers who had been engaged in the military service of the United States."

GEORGE'S GHOST

According to legend, George Colee is the resident ghost there. As the story goes, George had this home built in 1879 for his fiancée, Marina. Before the home was completed, Marina left George for a soldier named Wade, who was stationed at nearby Fort Marion. One evening, George approached Wade in the street and an altercation ensued. The two had words, and things ended there. A few weeks later, George's body was found dead in the bathtub upstairs in his home, with the cause of death listed as drowning and possibly by suicide. As the story unfolded, however, the police became suspicious of Marina and Wade. An investigation began, but there just wasn't enough evidence to convict the couple, and the murder was never solved. When the restaurant was opened in 1979, an article in the local newspaper reported that an old claw-foot tub had been found in an upstairs bathroom during renovations and was used as the salad bar for the restaurant. This would have been the same bathtub where George Colee died. To this day, the tub sits in the upstairs bar on the second floor of the restaurant.

When the home was converted into a restaurant, the old bathtub was used as the salad bar.

This is a very intriguing ghost story, but unfortunately it couldn't possibly be true. While the house was built in 1879 as the story states, it was built for George and his son William Colee, not for a woman named Marina. Also, George died a few months after construction began on the house, on August 5, 1879, at the home of his youngest son, Charles, who lived with his family in the community of Bakersville, located about 12 miles west of St. Augustine. His cause of death was old age—not suicide or murder—and he didn't die in the home in a bathtub. George's son, George A. Colee, was the owner of the home where Casa de Suenos now sits, which was in the previous story.

After George's death, his son William continued to live in the house until 1923. William was a tinner, blacksmith, and wheelwright. By 1924, Sidney Colee, a fisherman, is listed as the resident of the home along with his wife, Annie. The home became vacant during the 1930s up until the early 1940s, and by 1945, Leo Colee acquired it. In 1979, two business partners, Kevin Finch and Barry Gaines, bought the building. After extensive renovations, they opened Scarlett O'Hara's Restaurant that same year.

GENTLEMAN GEORGE

Although George Colee didn't die in the building, he is the name given for the male presence that haunts the home. Strange activity occurs throughout the building, but most of it happens in the second-floor bar. George likes to turn the upstairs lights on and off, especially when someone in the room mentions his name. According to Jasmine Staples, one of the restaurant's managers, George doesn't like it when men in the bar mistreat women. He has been known to push men who yell at their girlfriends or who use foul language, and any male acting up in the bar would encounter the wrath of George.

A few months before our investigation there, Jasmine and another employee took a trip to visit the nearby psychic town of Cassadega. As soon as Jasmine had sat down with a medium and before she could even speak, the first thing the medium asked her was "Who is George?" George Colee, whom the home was built for, is supposedly who haunts Scarlett O'Hara's. It was amazing that the psychic picked up on this name of all names, and he is the one tied to where she works. The psychic then asked Jasmine, "Do you trust George?" She said that she felt that George was protecting her, but that she needed to trust him. She said that if Jasmine didn't trust him, then to leave him alone. She also told Jasmine not to eat any food from the restaurant, because George was doing something to her food.

On many nights, while by herself in the office closing up, Jasmine will hear the sound of multiple voices talking to each other when no one else is in the building. The words are always too soft to decipher, but it is the distinct sound of multiple people talking all around her. Christina, one of the daytime employees,

The spirit of George does not like hostile guests.

has witnessed glasses flying off the shelves by themselves. She also reports that on several occasions she hears voices talking in the building when no one else is there. Most times it is a woman's voice she hears. Christina also sees doors in the office slam shut by themselves, and according to her, light switches turn themselves on and off in the building quite regularly.

Other female employees have felt the distinct feeling of someone blowing on their necks, which they always attribute to the ghost of George. Every year at Christmas, the staff will pour a shot of Jack Daniels and place it on the bar for George just before locking up for the night. The next morning when they come in, the shot glass is always empty.

THE INVESTIGATION

When our team was given the green light to investigate Scarlett O'Hara's, I jumped at the chance. This place had been at the top of my list of locations I wanted to investigate in St. Augustine. I arrived on a quiet Sunday night with one of my fellow investigators. When we arrived that evening, we were greeted by Jasmine, who then informed us that the building had been very active lately, and we should be in for a good night. As soon as we were walking up the stairs to the second-floor bar, Jasmine was mentioning that the lights turn on and off by themselves. Once we reached the second floor, the lights near the bar turned off by themselves, almost as if on cue. We had just arrived, and we were already experiencing activity!

As soon as we began our first EVP session at the second-floor bar, I asked, "Do you hate bad language?" An EVP was then captured of a deep male voice that responded with "Great." I feel as if this may have been the ghost of George agreeing to hating bad language. A little while later, my investigator and I were talking about the possibility that the male spirit haunting the restaurant wasn't really George Colee, but maybe a different person altogether. Right afterward, one of our audio recorders picked up an EVP of a gruff male voice that huffed with a heavy "hmmpphhh" sound. Maybe this was the grumpy male spirit who haunts the building.

A little while later during the same EVP session, I asked, "Who's pushing people?" Shortly afterward, my audio recorder picked up an EVP that responded with "Me." Less than two minutes later, the same gruff male voice was caught on the recording that said, "Him, out." We began to get the feeling that this male entity was not happy about us being there, and I was starting to feel that we may have worn out our welcome. This became more apparent when another EVP was caught about ten minutes later of the same voice, which said, "Spook them." Something was trying to scare us out of there, but we continued with the investigation. Throughout the rest of the night, things in the old building remained quiet. I was amazed, however, that we might have come in direct contact with the ghost of George Colee, or whoever the male spirit was that was known to haunt the bar.

Every time I am in St. Augustine, I always make a stop by Scarlett O'Hara's for a quick lunch and a cold draft beer. Although they have quite a few great menu items, I am somewhat partial to Kaye's Meatloaf Sandwich. The meatloaf is house-made, wrapped in bacon and served on toasted ciabatta bread with a spicy tomato aioli. This is good old-fashioned southern comfort food at its best. If you decide to visit, don't forget to make a quick trip to the upstairs bar, where they still have the old claw-foot tub on display. Make sure to watch your language, though, because George doesn't like anyone with a foul mouth.

CHAPTER 7

THE OLD INDIAN VILLAGE:

The Tolomato Cemetery Investigation

The Tolomato Cemetery sits over the site of an old Guale Indian village.

Just around the corner from the Potter's Wax Museum, along the north end of Cordova Street, sits the Tolomato Cemetery. Although the oldest burial here is of sixteen-year-old Elizabeth Forrester, who died in 1798, the land itself dates back much further. The earliest mention of Tolomato is in the year 1705, when the land was the site of an old Indian village and church. They were of the Guale Indians, who had arrived in St. Augustine from Georgia sometime during the sixteenth century, after several attacks from other hostile tribes had chased them from their land. After attacks on St. Augustine from the British forces in South Carolina and Georgia destroyed many of the Florida missions, they settled on this site in the early 1700s. The Franciscan Indian mission established on this site was named Nuestra Señora de Guadalupe de Tolomato, or Our Lady of Guadalupe of Tolomato. Although it is not known for sure, it is believed that the name Tolomato was derived from the name of a place or a river where they had originally come from.

THE MINORCANS

In 1765, a British physician, Dr. Andrew Turnbull, founded a colony in the New World in East Florida, which he decided to name New Smyrna, after his wife's birthplace in the ancient Greek city of Smyrna. The colony was located about 62 miles south of St. Augustine. Two years later, in 1767, he arrived in the Mediterranean with several ships, on which he enlisted over 1,400 colonists to aid him in the settlement of the new colony. The majority of these indentured servants were from the island of Minorca, located just off the coast of Spain. They were led by their spiritual leader, Father Pedro Camps of Minorca, along with his assistant, Father Bartolome Casanovas.

After arriving in the new colony, they worked on the plantations growing indigo, hemp, and sugar cane, which were used to make rum. Not long after they arrived there, Turnbull, who was seldom there, left the newly arrived colonists under the care of very cruel overseers. These poor people were worked to the bone and horribly mistreated. In 1777, after years of mistreatment and abuse, they were led by Father Pedro Camps on a long journey to St. Augustine. As soon as they arrived, they were granted asylum by the British governor Patrick Tonyn, who also gave them permission to bury their deceased in the "Old Catholic Cemetery" of Tolomato. Although it is more than likely that there are Indian burials there, this was the beginning of the use of Tolomato solely as a cemetery.

Tolomato Cemetery contains many burials, including the graves of several former American Black enslaved people, who had converted to Catholicism after escaping from slavery in the Carolinas. Others buried there included numerous

The first bishop of St. Augustine, Augustin Verot, is buried in the mortuary chapel at the back of the cemetery.

graves of Confederate soldiers who fought in the Civil War, as well as Father Miguel O'Reilly, who was the first pastor of what is now the Cathedral Basilica.

In 1853, Father Felix Varela died and was buried in a large white mortuary chapel toward the back of the cemetery. Born in Havana, Cuba, and raised in St. Augustine, Florida, Varela served in Spain and then later New York City, where he eventually rose to the title of vicar general of the Diocese of New York. After suffering from severe asthma, he returned to St. Augustine in 1848, where he eventually died five years later. Upon his death, he was buried in the Tolomato Cemetery. His remains were disinterred over sixty years later, and he was reburied in his hometown of Havana, Cuba. He was so diligent in his work with the church that he is currently being considered for canonization as a saint, and he has been declared a Servant of God.

Many people have reported seeing the apparition of a tall, dark figure wearing a dark-hooded cloak roaming the cemetery late at night. It is believed that this is the ghost of Father Felix Varela, clothed in his priestly robes and wandering the grounds.

A GRUESOME END

In 1870, Bishop Augustin Verot arrived in Florida to serve as the first bishop of St. Augustine. He had served previously in Paris, France, as well as in Baltimore, Maryland. From 1861 until 1870, when he relocated to St. Augustine, Verot served as the third bishop of the Diocese of Savannah, Georgia. When he died in St. Augustine in 1876, just six short years after his arrival there, he was buried in the Tolomato Cemetery. Because of his well-known stature, people came from far and wide to pay their respects to him. This included travelers who had to journey for a few weeks to make it to the funeral.

To put his corpse on display so that everyone could pay their respects, he was supposedly placed in a coffin that was packed with ice to preserve him. Since this soon started to get really messy, he was then placed in a sealed metal coffin with a small glass window over his face, so that everyone could see him one last time. Because he died in June, during the heat of the summer, decomposition began to set in fast. A few days later, during the bishop's funeral, the coffin began to make a loud hissing and gurgling sound. All of a sudden, the bishop's body exploded, sending chunks of his remains and bodily fluids all over the attendants of the funeral. Ever since then, he has been known as the exploding priest. It has been said that he "went out with a bang," and that he now "rests in pieces."

Although we do know that Bishop Verot was a very well-known priest in his time and that his funeral was attended by many parishioners, there is no record of the exploding-body incident happening—but it does make for a great story. With his death occurring as late as 1876, there would have been some record of the incident or a mention of it in the newspaper if it did indeed happen. The bishop was, however, interred in the mortuary chapel along with the remains of Father Felix Varela until Varela's body was disinterred years later and reburied in Havana, Cuba. Verot's remains are still in the chapel.

Interestingly enough, the same story about the exploding body has been told about the funeral of the ruler William the Conqueror. As the legend goes, his corpse burst all over everyone attending his funeral. Although the true story is slightly less gruesome, it is still disturbing in its own right. According to Benedictine monk Orderic Vitalis, who wrote in his Ecclesiastical History (written in Normandy between 1114 and 1141 CE) detailing the life of William the Conqueror, the events happened much differently. He wrote that during burial, the body of William was "great in body and strong, tall in stature but not ungainly." When they went to place his body in the coffin, they realized that it was too large for the stone sarcophagus. His body was bloated and badly decayed. They tried to force the corpse into the coffin to make him fit, which caused "the swollen bowels [to] burst, and an intolerable stench assailed the nostrils of the bystanders and the whole crowd."

LITTLE JAMES MORGAN

The most famous spirit that haunts the Tolomato Cemetery is the ghost of little James Morgan. One afternoon, on November 28, 1877, James was playing in the large oak tree near the cemetery gates. This was his favorite tree to climb, and as he was climbing, James slipped, and he fell to his death by tumbling to the ground headfirst and instantly breaking his neck. Distraught with grief, his mother received special permission from the bishop to bury him beneath the same tree he loved to climb in life. His parents bought the plots around his grave as well, so that to this day he has the entire section to himself.

Little James Morgan has this section of the cemetery all to himself.

Many have seen the ghost of James still sitting in that same tree. A few years ago, a young mother was visiting Tolomato Cemetery with her five-year-old daughter one afternoon. Her daughter had wandered off, and the mother found her beneath James's tree, jabbering away. When the mother asked the child who she was talking to, she replied, "Just the little boy who lives here." The mother quickly grabbed her child and left. Also, many guests taking photographs have captured what appears to be the ghost of James sitting in that same tree.

In 1884, both the Tolomato Cemetery and the nearby Huguenot Cemetery closed to burials for good. All the cemeteries within the city limits closed in that year, because it was believed at that time that the decomposition of bodies near residential areas, even if buried beneath the earth, aided in the spread of yellow fever. This dreadful disease had taken its toll on many of St. Augustine's residents over the years, and the city was doing whatever it could to prepare for another outbreak of the disease. It wasn't until the year 1905, due to the diligent work of Dr. Walter Reed, that the mosquito was identified as the carrier of the disease.

THE INVESTIGATION

The cemetery is now open to the public only on the third Saturday of every month, from 11:00 a.m. until 3:00 p.m. All other days the gates remain closed to visitors. With such limited access, I was absolutely speechless when I learned that I would be allowed to investigate this historic location. There were so many layers of history attached to the land, and I had high hopes of communicating with multiple entities during the investigation. Unfortunately, however, there was no paranormal evidence caught during the investigation. I must admit, there was an ominous feeling as I walked among the well-worn headstones and monuments, but I wasn't able to document anything out of the ordinary with my equipment.

Although I didn't capture any evidence, that doesn't mean that the cemetery isn't haunted. This is always one of the nightly stops on our St. Augustine ghost tour, and many of our guests have captured strange photographs in what is known as James Morgan's tree. Some have caught a small dark shadow nestled in the branches, while yet others have reported seeing a small little boy sitting in the neck of the tree, staring back at them and grinning. Whether it is the ghost of little James Morgan or the apparition of Father Felix Varela walking its grounds, the Tolomato Cemetery has been the location of many spectral sightings by many people over the years. Perhaps one day I will be lucky enough to capture my own paranormal evidence from this amazing location. Until then, I will be sure to pass by it every time I visit the city to pay my respects to James Morgan and the rest of the souls that inhabit the place.

THE THREE "RS":

The Oldest Wooden Schoolhouse Investigation

The Oldest Wooden Schoolhouse still has the chain that was wrapped around it in 1937 to help anchor the home to the ground from a hurricane.

In a town known as the oldest city in the United States, there are quite a few places that claim to be the first. The Oldest Wooden Schoolhouse, located on St. George Street, is no different. Labeled as the "Oldest Wooden Schoolhouse in America," this building has been sitting on the same lot for over two hundred years, ever since 1800. Unfortunately, this is not the oldest wooden schoolhouse in America. The oldest one is on Long Island, New York, and it is named the "Voorlezer's House," dating back to 1695. In all actuality, this is most likely the fourth- or fifth-oldest wooden schoolhouse in America.

Although property records for the land date back to 1740, the current structure that sits here was built sometime between 1800 and 1810 for a man named Juan Genopoly. Juan purchased the lot for sixty-eight pesos, and the house was built out of red cedar and cypress. Everything was made by hand, including the nails that hold it all together. Juan Genopoly was Greek by birth and a carpenter by trade. He arrived in St. Augustine in 1777 along with the Menorcan survivors of the New Smyrna colony. After arriving in St. Augustine, Genopoly turned to farming and leased land north of the Castillo, where he, along with his three enslaved workers, raised garden crops.

THE SCHOOL IS OPENED

Not long after his house was built, Genopoly began teaching Menorcan children to read, write, and do arithmetic. As time went on, his wife, as well as two of his children, also became teachers at this small school. The school continued to operate there until the last class was held in 1864. Throughout the next few years, the home was handed down to Juan Genopoly's children, and later his grandchild John Darling acquired the building after his mother's death in 1884. John was a Confederate veteran of the Civil War, and he was a gunsmith by trade. He also owned a small curio shop on the corner of Treasury and Charlotte Streets, just a few blocks away. By 1907, Thomas Kearns and his wife, Cora, opened a curio shop in the house. The Kearnses were the first to begin calling the home "the Old, Old Schoolhouse." By the 1920s, it had become Miss Erwin's Red Cedar Tea House and then the Old Cedar Schoolhouse Restaurant. In 1931, plans to convert the home into a museum began. In that same year, nine students from the class of 1864 visited the schoolhouse. It was the first time they had been there in nearly seventy years. During their visit, they rearranged the desks and the furniture to be as they remembered it during their school days, making the museum as authentic as possible to the original Genopoly schoolhouse.

A few years after the old schoolhouse opened to the public as a museum, a major hurricane hit St. Augustine (in 1937). In an attempt to keep the home from flying away during the storm, townspeople wrapped a huge chain around the building and secured it to a large anchor. Over half a century later, the chain and anchor remain attached to the building.

STRANGE OCCURRENCES

Ever since its opening to the public, the Oldest Wooden Schoolhouse hasn't failed to disappoint when it comes to hauntings. Several of the staff have reported seeing the ghosts of soldiers and sailors walking around inside the schoolhouse. As with other locations in this book, the lot sits near the site where construction workers who were building the Castillo de San Marcos lived in the late 1600s, so this may account for those strange apparitions.

When children misbehaved at school, the were locked in a small room that sits under the staircase.

During the schoolhouse years, when the children were really bad they would be locked in a tiny room under the staircase nicknamed "the dungeon." They would be forced to stay in those cramped quarters until they could learn to behave. There have been reports of the child dummy that sits in that tiny room moving on its own and tapping on the clear Plexiglas window. Other forms of punishment included paddling, as well as wearing the dunce cap.

The second floor of the schoolhouse is off-limits to the public due to safety concerns, but that doesn't stop numerous visitors from trying to sneak up there to take a look around. One time a man snuck up there after being told no, and he was pushed down the stairs by what he described as an elderly woman dressed as an old schoolmarm. When he looked back up the staircase, there was no one there. Others have reported hearing and seeing the ghosts of little children roaming throughout the building. Furthermore, the main schoolroom is full of animatronic schoolchildren and an animatronic schoolmaster that are known to turn on and move by themselves.

THE INVESTIGATION

To say that I wasn't the least bit apprehensive about investigating a room filled with creepy animatronic dolls would be a lie. The home had an even more ominous presence after all the visitors and staff had left and it began to get dark. On the other hand, both my wife, Kim, and I were very excited as we were accompanied by our two daughters, Jennifer and Addison, and this was to be their very first paranormal investigation. We were joined by Stephen Tighe, who is an investigator with REAP Paranormal, out of the northeastern Pennsylvania area.

The animatronic headmaster and school children have moved on their own from time to time, even when they are turned off. Photo by Kim Dunn

A little over an hour into the investigation, all of us were in the main school room conducting an EVP session. All of a sudden, we captured an EVP of a male spirit that growled, "You should go." It seemed that he wasn't too happy we were there investigating that night. A few seconds later, a second EVP was caught. This time it was a voice that said, "There's something in there." We asked a few questions in response to see what this entity was referring to, but we didn't receive an answer.

Another chilling EVP that was captured during our investigation was in response to a question that Stephen asked: "What are we here for?" An EVP was then picked up that responded with "A woman." Maybe they were referring to the ghost of the old school marm that is known to haunt the place.

During our investigation that night, we managed to capture a few other EVPs, as well as multiple unexplainable spikes on our EMF detectors. In addition, the old building itself was downright creepy at night. I personally was rather pleased that none of the animatronic dolls started up by themselves and that the small child in the case underneath the stairs stayed put. (I had already dealt with haunted dolls at the Antiques and Uniques store on Aviles Street, and that was more than enough for me.) Overall, the case was a success, and we look forward to working with Stephen and his team on future investigations.

Although it claims to be the oldest wooden schoolhouse in America, it is most likely the fourth- or fifth-oldest schoolhouse in the country.

The Oldest Wooden Schoolhouse is open to visitors seven days a week from 10:00 a.m. until 5:00 p.m., and until 7:00 p.m. on Fridays and Saturdays. They even give you a small diploma after the tour, which is a neat addition. Although it may not technically be the oldest wooden schoolhouse in America as it claims, it definitely holds its place in St. Augustine's rich history. In addition, it is among the top five oldest wooden schoolhouses in our country, and that in itself is a proud title to hold.

The Potter's Wax Museum Investigation

Potter's Wax Museum is one of the most haunted locations in St. Augustine.

This two-story frame building that sits along the corner of Cordova and Orange Streets was constructed in 1886. Its earliest occupant is listed as Speissigger Drug Store in 1887, which was owned and operated by a man named T. W. Speissigger, a druggist from Charleston, South Carolina. He arrived in St. Johns County in 1868, and by 1875 he had purchased a drugstore from Barola Genovar and J. D. Lopez. After his second location burned down in the 1887 fire, he moved his business to the current site. A listing in the 1911 city directory advertises the store as selling "Drugs, special agents, Pratt Food Co.'s Products, Hawks lenses, Dr. Buckthorn's splits, Weeks cold tablets," as well as many other medicines. Many of the drugs sold in those days would be considered unsafe by today's standards, and numerous old medicine bottles sold at the store during that time are on display today at Potter's in the old drugstore.

Throughout the next few years, Speissigger operated his drugstore downstairs and ran a boardinghouse on the second floor of the building. In 1927, he handed the business down to his two sons, T. Julius Speissigger and R. Alston Speissigger. Julius was the druggist for the company, and Alston was a veterinarian surgeon and practiced in the building. Throughout the 1930s and until the 1960s, it was used by the Speissigger brothers as a drugstore and sundries shop. Many schoolchildren from the nearby school used to stop by the store for penny candy after classes let out for the day. They continued to operate there until the 1960s, when it became the Old Authentic Drug Store Museum. In 2014, Potter's Wax Museum moved into the building. Potter's had originally been located at 1 King Street from 1948 to 1986 and at 17 King Street from 1987 to 2013.

The Speissigger brothers operated their drugstore here throughout the late 1800s and early 1900s.

The front room of Potter's Wax Museum is set up to resemble the old drugstore.

WAX ON, WAX OFF

George L. Potter originally established the wax collection in 1948, and it is the oldest wax museum in the United States. As a young child, George traveled the world with his family. After a trip to London, where he visited Madame Tussaud's Wax Museum, he developed a love for the art. As an adult, after making his fortune in real estate, he decided to follow his dream and open the first wax museum in America. Since his death in 1979, the museum has continued to operate until this day. The current museum houses over 150 wax sculptures, including many historical figures as well as pop icons, with everything from US presidents to Rambo and Freddy Krueger. They continue to make wax figures at this location, and it takes about a year to make one figure. Real human hair is used in the process, as well as medical-grade prosthetics for the eyes and the teeth. One would wonder how they don't melt here in the Florida heat, but according to the staff, it would take a heat of at least 150°F to melt them—and they also leave the air-conditioning running constantly.

Ever since Potter's moved into the building in 2014, there have been numerous reports by employees and visitors of hauntings there. Many have reported seeing wax figures turn their heads and move on their own, and jars have been known to fly off the shelves by themselves in the old drugstore area. Interestingly enough, the building that houses Potter's Wax Museum sits over the top of a portion of the old Tolomato Cemetery, and where the parking lot is located used to be an old Spanish mission. There is a very good chance that this building is sitting on top of bodies from the old burying ground, which may account for some of the hauntings that have occurred there.

It takes approximately one year to make just one of the wax figures here.

THE INVESTIGATION

When I finally received the opportunity to investigate there, I was thrilled. This would be my first time investigating a wax museum, and, I have to admit, I was a little bit apprehensive. The idea of roaming around the dark with over 150 wax sculptures staring back at me seemed a little much. I don't frighten easily, but I have to concede that I am not a huge fan of mannequins, lifelike full-size sculptures, or anything similar, and this place was filled with them.

Not long after arriving, before turning the lights out, I rounded the corner and witnessed the head on the Galileo figure turn about 30 degrees and stare directly back at me. Now it would be one thing if I saw this out of the corner of my eye, since these things are very lifelike, but I was staring directly at it when it happened! This caught me completely off guard, and it took me a little while to collect myself. After I finished setting up, I couldn't believe I was about to be in the dark alone with these figures.

In order to keep their lifelike appearance, real human hair is used when making the wax figures.

Throughout the investigation, I could feel hundreds of eyes watching me, and I felt that at any moment one of the figures would reach out and try to grab me. Of course, I knew it was my own mind making the worst of the situation, but that didn't make it any better. After I turned my audio recorder on, one of the first questions that I asked was "Are the Speissigger brothers here?" I received an immediate response of a voice that answered with "No." A little while later, I received another EVP that may have shed some light on who or what may be haunting the place. I asked, "Are you tied to the Tolomato Cemetery that was beneath this building?" An EVP was then captured that answered, "They left me for dead." Maybe this was the spirit of one of the people who were still buried in Tolomato Cemetery.

One of the creepiest pieces of audio evidence caught that night happened as I was walking past the wax sculpture of Henry Flagler. Just as I passed by, my recorder picked up an EVP of a voice that said, "There he is." At least one of these entities was aware of my presence there, and it was an intelligent spirit. As the investigation pressed on, the feeling of being watched seemed to increase. I still couldn't get used to all the figures surrounding me. As I wrapped things up, I can say that I was more than happy that the investigation was over. I felt as though I couldn't get out of there fast enough. There is a strange feeling in this building, and whatever it is that haunts the place continues to make its presence known.

CHAPTER 10

A BEACON FOR THE SPIRITS:

The St. Augustine Lighthouse Investigation

There have been several recorded deaths at the St. Augustine Lighthouse, which may account for all the haunted activity there.

Just a short drive across the historic Bridge of Lions, on Anastasia Island, sits the St. Augustine Lighthouse. Although its beacon has been navigating ships through treacherous waters since 1874, similar structures existed there many years before. A map of the raid on St. Augustine that took place in 1568, led by Sir Henry Drake, shows a Spanish watchtower existing on Anastasia Island. By 1683, a coquina lighthouse tower was built that was created from the remains of an old stone chapel. This structure survived until 1880, when it finally fell into the sea due to erosion.

In 1859, just a few short decades before the original tower succumbed to the sea, lighthouse keeper Joseph Andreu fell to his death while whitewashing the structure. According to the December 10, 1859, issue of the St. Augustine Examiner, he "first struck the roof of the oil room about thirty feet below, whence he glanced off and struck the stone wall which encloses the Light House, and thence to the ground . . . killing him instantly." By 1870, it was realized that the watchtower would soon succumb to erosion, so the US Congress appropriated funds for a new lighthouse.

In June 1872, Hezekiah Pittee was selected to oversee construction of the new tower. During construction on the lighthouse, Pittee moved his entire family from Maine to live on-site while it was being built. To easily transport supplies from the beach up to the tower, a rail cart was installed that ran the length of the distance between the two. His five children were frequently known to ride the cart back and forth on the tracks just for fun. A little over a year after construction began, in July 1873, tragedy struck.

A HORRIFIC OCCURRENCE

One day, a few of Pittee's children, along with a young daughter of one of the workers, were riding the cart. As it came down toward the beach, the mechanism that was supposed to stop the cart at the end of the track failed, and the children, as well as the cart, were thrown from the track and into the murky sea. The heavy iron cart fell on top of the children and pinned them underneath the water. Two of them were able to escape, but two of Pittee's daughters, Mary, age fifteen, and Eliza, age thirteen, as well as the worker's young daughter, drowned.

Over the years, visitors to the lighthouse have reported seeing two soaking-wet young girls, pale in complexion and covered in seaweed, walking near the beach and believed to be the ghosts of Mary and Eliza Pittee. Many paranormal investigators who have visited the lighthouse have also reported hearing the sound of little girls crying in the tower.

A year later, in 1874, work was finally completed on the new lighthouse. Containing more than one million individual bricks and standing at 165 feet, this opposing structure was 95 feet taller than the previous watchtower. By 1880, the previous watchtower finally fell into the ocean due to erosion. It is now an underwater archeological site.

On August 31, 1886, the Charleston earthquake shook the lighthouse so badly that, according to the keeper's log, the tall tower swayed violently back and forth for a full forty seconds before finally settling. But, amazingly, there was no reported damage. Nearly three years later, on May 31, 1889, lighthouse keeper William Harn died in the keeper's house after a long battle with tuberculosis. There have been many reports of employees hearing the sound of an old man coughing in the keeper's house hours after its closing, which is believed to be the ghost of William Harn still roaming the home in which he died.

CATS WITH PARACHUTES

In 1935, Cardell D. Daniels was appointed head keeper of the lighthouse. He moved into the keeper's house with his wife and two children: his son, Cracker, and his daughter, Wilma. One afternoon, Cracker wanted to see if cats could float, so he attached a parachute to his sister's cat, Smokey. He then dropped the cat off the top of the lighthouse. Thankfully, the cat landed without injury, but the animal was extremely frightened after the incident and went missing for several weeks. It wasn't until over fifty years later, during a visit to their childhood home at the old lighthouse, that he finally told his sister about the event.

Unfortunately, in 1970 the keeper's house was almost destroyed in a fire that was caused by an unknown arsonist. A decade later, a group known as the Junior Service League of St. Augustine began a campaign to restore the old building to its original splendor. Eighteen years later, in March 1988, restoration of the keeper's house was complete, and the Lighthouse Museum was opened to the public. In 1999, LAMP (the Lighthouse Archaeological Maritime Program) was founded. They are committed to studying the artifacts found in the waters right off the coast, many of which are on display in the museum located in the keeper's house. To this day, they continue to conduct archeological dives of shipwrecks off the coast of Anastasia Island and the surrounding areas.

In 2006, the Atlantic Paranormal Society (TAPS) crew from SyFy Channel's Ghost Hunters television show investigated the lighthouse for their season 2, episode 19, segment, which aired in May of that year. During their investigation, they were able to capture one of the best pieces of video evidence that they have ever picked up on camera. During the case, one of their infrared cameras caught the apparition of a dark figure looking down at them from the top of the lighthouse tower. It leaned over the rail and peered down at them, and then it moved back and disappeared. This piece of video evidence, as well as the apparition that they caught on video in the basement of the Moon River Brewing Company in Savannah, Georgia, are two of the best pieces of evidence ever captured by the TAPS crew.

THE INVESTIGATION

As soon as we arrived for the investigation, I was immediately drawn to the lighthouse tower. I had been to the museum before, so I was fairly familiar with the surroundings. For some strange reason, I felt that I had to go up to the top of the lighthouse as soon as we got there. Upon entering the tower, I immediately turned on my digital recorder and began ascending the spiral staircase that led up to the top. While I was walking up the stairs, a chilling EVP was instantly picked up on the audio recorder that said, "Come here." Was this entity beckoning me to come farther? Maybe the spirit was what was causing me to want to head to the top of the tower.

When I was about a quarter of the way up, I began to feel extremely dizzy and disoriented. I have never had a problem with vertigo before, and this seemed to come out of nowhere. I ascended a few more stairs, and the higher I got, the worse the feeling became. I knew that if I went any farther, things would become more dangerous. Begrudgingly, I decided to head back down to ground level and exit the tower to collect myself. As soon as I was outside again, everything was fine, and I felt okay. Later during the investigation, I reentered the tower several times and even went to the top on a couple of occasions, and that strange feeling never returned.

As soon as I exited the tower after my bout with vertigo, I began replaying the audio. Right before the wave of dizziness began to affect me, my audio recorder captured an unsettling EVP of a deep male voice that growled, "Get out." It was immediately afterward that I began to experience the feeling of vertigo. I feel that perhaps one of the entities was trying to lead me up to the top of the lighthouse, while another, more malevolent spirit didn't want me in the structure.

Later on into the investigation, I was walking along the small trail in the woods that winds around the lighthouse grounds. All of a sudden I began to hear small footsteps walking behind me. I stopped and turned around, but there was no one there. As I began walking down the path once more, I could again hear the sound of these phantom footsteps. Once more I turned around and looked behind me, and again I was all alone in the woods. At about the same time that this occurred, my audio recorder captured an EVP of a small child's laughter coming from directly behind me. Had I possibly had an encounter with the ghost of one of the children who died in the rail cart accident many years before? Even scarier, I wasn't far from where the spirits of the dead ghost children had been sighted coming out of the water and walking along the beach.

There is most definitely a spiritual presence at the St. Augustine Lighthouse, and it appears that the place is haunted by multiple entities, some of which are intelligent ghosts. It is very likely that the two Pittee children, along with their friend, who died in the cart accident still haunt these grounds. Perhaps the male entity that people have encountered over the years is the ghost of a previous lighthouse keeper, most likely either Joseph Andreu or William Harn. With such a tragic history, it is no wonder that the St. Augustine Lighthouse is known to be one of Florida's most haunted locations.

CHAPTER II

IF THESE WALLS COULD TALK:

The Castillo de San Marcos Investigation

The Castillo de San Marcos is the oldest masonry fort in the continental United States.

Jutting out along the Matanzas River, as silent as a sentinel guarding the waterway into the city, the Castillo de San Marcos is the oldest masonry fortress in the United States. Its massive walls are over 10 feet thick at the base, and they taper up to over 30 feet high. The fort has four bastions located at each of its four corners, which are named the San Pedro, San Agustín, San Carlos, and San Pablo bastions. Its walls were built out of coquina, which was quarried from nearby Anastasia Island. Coquina, which in Spanish means "small shells," is made up of tiny seashells that have bonded together over many years to form a porous sedimentary rock. These rocks were formed into bricks that were then used to build the fort. At the time, this was the only stone available for construction in the area. Due to its porous nature, the coquina walls of the fort were able to absorb cannon balls as opposed to cracking when hit by enemy fire.

THE HISTORY

After an attack on the city of St. Augustine in 1668 by English pirate Robert Searle, in which most of the city was burned to the ground, the need for a strong masonry fortification was realized. In 1672, after construction was finally approved, work began on the Castillo de San Marcos. Designed by Spanish engineer Ignacio Daza, most of the labor on the fort was done by Native Americans from nearby Spanish missions, as well as from workers brought in from Havana, Cuba. Although construction on the fort began in 1672, it wasn't until twenty-three years later, in 1695, that it was finally completed.

A PIRATE'S LIFE FOR ME

In fall of 1684, English pirate Andrew Ranson's ship, the Cagway, landed just off the coast of St. Augustine. Ranson and six of his men boarded a small boat and went ashore to try to trade with the local Timucua Indians for food and supplies. As soon as they stepped on land, they were arrested by two Spanish soldiers and placed in a jail located in the partially finished Castillo de San Marcos. At first, Ranson would not admit to being a pirate. It wasn't until he was tied over a cannon and brutally lashed repeatedly with a whip that he finally confessed. Governor Cabrera, the leader of the area at that time, found Ranson and his men guilty of piracy and sentenced them to execution by garroting. Garroting is a form of execution in which the condemned person is forced to sit in a seat against a post or tree, while a thick rope is placed around their neck. The executioner will then take a stout stick and twist the rope from behind the victim until it becomes tighter and tighter, eventually strangling them.

On the day of his execution, Ranson and his crew were led from the jail at the fort to the plaza to be garroted. To make his punishment even worse, the governor ordered Ranson to watch all six of his men executed first, witnessing the whole gruesome ordeal. When Ranson's turn came, the rope around his neck was twisted tighter and tighter. Just before he lost consciousness, the rope snapped, and he gasped with air. Father Perez de la Mota, who was the priest on-site to perform the last rites, declared it as a sign from God and granted Ranson sanctuary within the church.

Governor Cabrera, who was highly upset with the outcome of the event, claimed that the rope used to garrote Ranson must have been old and rotted, and he immediately sent word to Rome to get the sanctuary claim dismissed. In the meantime, the governor concocted a new plan. Ranson had apprenticed as a stone mason years before in England, and the fort was in the process of being built. The governor told Ranson that he would spare his life if he would assist in the fort's construction. Ranson then became assistant to the chief engineer of the fort. When the fort was attacked by the English in 1702, Ranson helped the Spanish in fighting the British. He actually took up arms against his home country to save his own neck! By that year, he had already been married into a family here in St. Augustine, and he was pretty well established.

SIEGE OF 1702

In November 1702, the English attacked St. Augustine, laying siege to the city. The entire town of nearly 1,500 people was walled up inside the fort during the attack. The worst of the fighting came a few weeks later, on November 25, when a twenty-four-hour gun battle ensued, with both the British and the Spanish setting fire to sections of the city to clear lanes for firing. By late December, Spanish reinforcements arrived from Havana, Cuba, with four Spanish man-of-war ships. The British then gave up and retreated to South Carolina.

SIEGE OF 1740

In June 1740, General James Edward Oglethorpe, the founder of the English colony of Savannah, Georgia, arrived off the coast of St. Augustine with seven ships. During his siege on the city, the entire population of the town, along with its soldiers, once again walled themselves up within the fort. After nearly a month of attacks and no progress, Oglethorpe and his men were forced to retreat. Their cannon fire could not damage the walls of the Castillo de San Marcos, and they were beginning to run low on supplies. Hanging their heads in defeat, they returned to Georgia.

A few years later, in 1763, Florida came under British rule with the signing of the Treaty of Paris. It wasn't until 1784 that it was returned to the Spanish. During this period, three signers of the Declaration of Independence were imprisoned within its walls, as well as many other patriots. While under British rule, the fort was renamed Fort St. Mark, but it returned to its original name after the Spanish regained Florida. A few years later, in 1821, Florida became a US territory, and the Americans renamed the castillo Fort Marion, after the South Carolinian and Revolutionary War hero Francis Marion.

OSCEOLA'S HEAD

In October 1837, during the Second Seminole War, Seminole Indian chief Osceola was taken prisoner by the Americans while attending a peace conference near Fort Peyton under a flag of truce. He was imprisoned in Fort Marion along with his followers and many other prisoners. Osceola was later transferred to Fort Moultrie, South Carolina, where he died in January 1838 from malaria. It has been said that his skull was kept as a curio by his good friend Dr. Frederick Weedon, who decapitated Osceola after his death and kept the head in a preservative until it was later taxidermized. It was also said that when Dr. Weedon's children misbehaved at bedtime, he would tie Osceola's head from the bedpost of their bed to scare them into listening. There have been reports by visitors to the Castillo claiming to see a decapitated head floating around on its own, which is believed to be that of Osceola. There is no proof that Dr. Weedon removed Osceola's head after his death, but there is nothing to negate that it ever happened either.

From 1886 to 1887, approximately 491 Apache and Chiricahua Indians were held prisoner at the Castillo de San Marcos. Eighty-two were men, and the rest were women and children. Among these was the wife of the legendary Indian chief Geronimo, as well as many of his fellow tribesmen. While at the fort, many of the prisoners had to camp in small tents, since there was not sufficient space for all of them. At least twenty-four Apaches died during their incarceration there due to these poor living conditions, and their bodies were buried in North Beach.

In 1900, after 205 years in service, and serving under five different flags throughout its existence, the Castillo de San Marcos was taken off active duty as a military installation. A few decades later, in 1924, the fort was declared a national monument.

A SURPRISING DISCOVERY

One of the most famous stories about the Castillo de San Marcos concerns a gruesome tale about an officer named Colonel Garcia Marti, who was stationed there with his wife, Dolores. As the tale goes, the colonel's wife became smitten with a young officer named Captain Abela, who was also stationed at the fort. The two young lovers began to sneak around behind the colonel's back and developed an illustrious affair. When he discovered this, he had the pair chained to the walls of the powder magazine on the fort's interior, facing each other. They were then bricked up alive behind the walls for their adultery and forced to watch each other slowly die of starvation. Many years later, after the fort became a national park and tourist destination, a few of the fort employees were testing a heavy cannon. All of a sudden, the ground beneath the cannon gave way and a secret room was discovered. Who should they find but the skeletons of the two lovers still chained to the walls.

This is one heck of a great story, but according to park rangers at the fort, this never happened. First of all, no human remains were discovered in the powder magazine except the bones of one arm and a leg. There were other bones discovered, but they were animal bones. Looking at the fort's history, only three years after construction the powder magazine was declared useless because of its inadequate ventilation. The room became the garbage bin of the fort for many years, and the animal bones were from the many livestock, swine, and other animals eaten by the fort's inhabitants during the sieges that occurred there. The human arm and leg found can be traced back as well. During the English attack on the fort in 1702, on November 10 of that year, a tragic accident occurred while soldiers were firing an old 16-pound iron cannon from the San Pablo bastion. The cannon exploded, killing three soldiers and injuring five more. One of the men ended up losing his arm, and another lost his leg; hence the human remains found in the garbage. In addition, there is no record of this affair/murder among the colonel, his wife, and the other officer.

I was first introduced to the existence of the Castillo de San Marcos from its airing on the Travel Channel's hit television show Ghost Adventures. It originally aired on June 12, 2009. for the season 2, episode 10 segment. During their investigation, they caught a video of what appeared to be a soldier at the top of the fort. He struck a few times, trying to light what appeared to be a lantern. It finally lit, and the soldier continued on his walk around the battlements of the fort. At the time that this video was captured, there was no one on the upper deck. Many visitors to the fort late at night have reported seeing a dark figure that appears to

This hidden room in the fort is one of its most haunted areas.

be a soldier walking along the battlements. This cannot be, because the fort closes at promptly 5:15 p.m., and the only way to get into the fort at that time would be to scale its massive 30-foot-high walls, which is virtually impossible.

The Castillo de San Marcos is at the top of the investigation wish list of any paranormal investigator wishing to conduct investigations in St. Augustine. With its tragic history and all the events that occurred there over the years, it is no wonder that this is one of the most haunted locations in the city, and perhaps in all of Florida. It is almost as if the fort's coquina walls have absorbed all the energy of everything that has happened there throughout its dark history.

THE INVESTIGATION

As soon as I arrived for the investigation that night, there was a strange feeling in the air. The entire town was very quiet, and a dead silence permeated the atmosphere. Even though the air was silent, the fort itself seemed very much alive. Throughout the whole investigation, I felt that I was being watched and that there was an unseen presence just around the corner, following my every move.

During our investigation of the fort, our team managed to capture an amazing Class A EVP, but strangely enough, the voice was in English. Although this is a Spanish fort, it was also occupied by English, American, and Confederate forces over its more than three-hundred-year history, so this could very well account for the language. Perhaps this is a residual haunting of one of those spirits. The EVP clearly said, "Ready! Fire!" This was also caught at around four in the morning, and none of our investigators heard it on location when it happened; it was heard only on the playback.

Throughout the rest of the investigation, things remained fairly quiet. I had hoped to capture the apparition of a soldier on one of our many infrared or thermal-imaging cameras, but I had no such luck. The EVP that was captured, though, was absolutely amazing, and although it cannot be scientifically documented, the overall feeling that pervaded the place was not to be discounted.

If you decide to visit St. Augustine, a trip would not be complete without a visit to the Castillo de San Marcos, since it is the oldest structure in the oldest city in America.

CHAPTER 12

AMMUNITION FOR A HAUNTING:
The Old Powder House Inn Investigation

The Old Powder House Inn is home to several ghosts, including the spirit of a little girl.

Nestled along Cordova Street in downtown St. Augustine sits the Old Powder House Inn. This beautiful home was built in 1899 for Eugene Segui, who was a druggist and the proprietor of the St. George Pharmacy, which was originally founded by Clarence A. Capo. Capo's wife, Catherine, owned Capo's Corset and Children's Shop, and she later lived in the home on Cordova Street after her husband died and Segui acquired the business. Segui died a few years later, leaving his wife, Mary, a widow. During that same period, a shrimper named Vincent J. Amato and his wife also lived in a portion of the house.

By 1954, the building had been converted into four separate apartments called Mary Francis Apartments. In 1968, Henry Paris purchased the building. He renamed it Paris Apartments about a year afterward. Throughout the next twenty-one years, it continued as Paris Apartments, with numerous tenants living there during that time. In 1989, it was converted into the Old Powder House Inn. The inn came by this unique name because it sat where a powder magazine originally was located and was used to store guns and ammunition for the colony. This existed there for many years before the home was built. A few decades later, the current owners, Bob and Suzanne Hailey, purchased the inn.

Ever since Bob and Suzanne Haley have had the inn, all manner of paranormal activity has occurred in the home. The previous owner loved to collect antique dolls, which she kept in the "Memories Room." Right after purchasing the place, Suzanne decided to place all the dolls in the bottom drawer of the secretary in the room because they gave her the creeps. On many occasions, housekeepers would come into the room and find the drawer open, and all the dolls would be laid out on the floor. This would occur even when no one was staying in the room, causing many maids to quit. Also, there are two decorative plates that hang on the wall in the room. One time a housekeeper came into the room to find the two plates sitting on the floor, and all the dolls were seated around them.

The ghost child in the Memories Room loves to play with the dolls there.

A CHILD GHOST

According to Bob, the previous owner told him that there was the ghost of a little girl that haunts the Memories Room, who would rearrange things that were on the shelves. This would happen even when no one was staying at the inn. The owner would fix them and place the items back in their original location, but when she would return the next morning, all the items would be moved around again. She finally decided to leave them where the little girl placed them. She figured that if that was where she wanted them, then that was where they would stay.

Guests staying in the Memories Suite will find that things go missing, only to turn up on the morning of checkout. They have also come into the room to find their things gone through and strung all over the place. This is thought to be the ghost of the little girl going through their belongings.

A few years ago, there were two ladies staying in the Queen Ann Room at the inn. They had just checked in and walked into their room. Hanging on one of the walls was a turn-of-the-twentieth-century portrait of a very stern-looking woman. The ladies didn't like the picture since it creeped them out, so they took it down and placed it on the floor, facing the wall, so they wouldn't have to look at it. After going back to their car to grab the rest of their luggage, they returned to the room to find the portrait hanging back on the wall. Bob said that they immediately ran downstairs and said, "We need a glass of wine now!"

THE INVESTIGATION

In early July 2019, our paranormal research team, the Savannah Ghost Research Society, was given overnight access to the inn to conduct an investigation. With all the paranormal encounters reported by staff and guests, I was sure that this place would not disappoint, and I sure wasn't wrong. This was to be the second investigation with my two daughters, Jennifer and Addison, and I was excited to have them along with me. Not long after we had arrived and set up all our equipment, we headed to the parlor to begin. As I was doing sweeps with our FLIR thermal-imaging camera, Addison suddenly felt extremely nauseated. She had to leave the room immediately. As soon as she left the room, she felt fine. When she later returned to the parlor, she began to feel sick again.

Throughout the investigation and for the rest of the night, all our evidence was captured in the Memories Room. The first incident happened after we returned from the parlor. As soon as we entered the room, I noticed that the television had been unplugged and pulled away from the wall. I immediately moved it back and plugged it back in. Later that night, after coming back into the room again, I found it once again unplugged. This happened later on for a third time, and this time there was also a small stuffed animal that had been placed in the room in the center on the floor.

During an EVP session in the Memories Room, I asked, "Are you upset that they took the dolls out of this room? Did you like to play with all the dolls?" An EVP was then captured of a little girl that replied, "I want a dollhouse!" Was this the spirit of the same little girl that is known to haunt the room? It certainly seemed so, and she was none too happy that her dolls had been taken away from her. Just before we left the room and headed upstairs, I decided to place a static recorder on the nightstand beside the bed and leave it running while we were gone. After later reviewing the audio, a very strange EVP was captured at that time of a male voice that said, "My tissues have taken over me. I want you to know. Listen to me." This is quite possibly the longest EVP that we have ever captured in almost ten years of paranormal investigations. Maybe this entity was trying to tell us what had happened to them in the afterlife. As the night went on, things seemed to quiet down, but we did manage to capture a few other pieces of evidence, but nothing like the first few EVPs that we caught.

I was amazed that during our investigation we were able to capture evidence of the little girl that haunts the Memories Room. This child's spirit still resides there, and she is very active. Many of our findings during the investigation coincided with the incidents described by Bob and Suzanne and their staff. If you decide to pay a visit to the Old Powder House Inn, I highly suggest staying in the Memories Room if you are looking for a ghostly encounter. If not, you may want to find other accommodations, since the spirits here like to make themselves known on a regular basis. They serve one of the best breakfasts that I have ever had at any inn. Their signature dish is called Eggs Cordova, which is a bacon cup filled with a poached egg and topped with their version of hollandaise sauce, served with homemade hash browns. Their concierge, Brian Taylor, also bakes homemade bread that is served with breakfast. Trust me, you will not be disappointed.

FALLEN HEROES:
The St. Augustine National Cemetery Investigation

The St. Augustine National Cemetery is the final resting place of nearly three thousand soldiers, including those who fought in the Seminole Wars, the Civil War, and World War II.

Although the land for the St. Augustine National Cemetery was designated in the year 1821, its history dates back much further. Prior to the burial ground existing there, this area was originally the site of a Franciscan monastery. During St. Augustine's British period, which lasted from 1763 until 1783, the monastery was occupied by the English troops. During the Second Spanish period, which was from 1783 until 1821, it remained in the hands of the Spanish military. The cemetery's first burial took place in 1828, and most of its earliest burials were from soldiers who had died in the Second Seminole War, which lasted from 1835 until 1842.

THE SECOND SEMINOLE WAR

After the passing of the Indian Removal Act of 1830 by the US government, Florida began the process of attempting to remove all the Seminole Indians from the state and relocating them to Indian territories located farther west. Tensions mounted as many of the natives refused to leave their sacred land, and it wasn't very long before a war ensued. As relations between the American government and the Seminole Indians deteriorated, the situation erupted into a war that lasted for seven years and was regarded as one of the longest and bloodiest conflicts with Native Americans that ever occurred in the United States.

THE DADE MASSACRE

On December 23, 1835, Major Francis Dade and his regiment of 110 troops and seven officers were ordered as reinforcements to Fort King, which was stationed in Ocala, Florida. Along the journey, Dade and his men soon became lost. Five days after they had first begun their trek, on December 28, they were ambushed by the Seminole Indians. Not long after the first shots rang out, Dade and all his men save three were massacred in the bloody battle. As the soldiers lay dying on the ground, the natives came through and butchered any of the remaining living.

Among the only survivors of the battle was Private Edward Decourcey, who had been hidden among a large pile of dead bodies, along with Ransom Clark, who had suffered five gunshot wounds and several large bleeding cuts to the head. A third soldier, Private Joseph Sprague, also survived the battle. The three were then pursued by the Seminoles, and Decourcey was also slaughtered. Of the two remaining survivors, only Clark was able to give a full account of the massacre and all that had happened, since Sprague was known to be illiterate. Dade and his men were later buried at the site of the slaughter.

Seven years later, in 1842, once hostilities had ceased, the remains of Major Francis Dade and his men were reinterred in the St. Augustine National Cemetery. Along with Major Dade and his men, the remains of other soldiers who died during the war were also interred there. The remains were placed in three separate graves, upon which were placed three large pyramids constructed out of coquina. Surrounding these pyramids are several plain white stone markers that were placed there to signify the Seminole Indian scouts. This was done on August 14, 1842, and it also marked the end of the Florida Indian Wars. The coquina pyramids were originally covered with white stucco, which has since worn away over the years. By 1881, the burial ground was declared a national cemetery. In that same year, the Dade Monument, which is a tall coquina stone obelisk, was erected to pay tribute to the sacrifice Dade and his men made in December 1835.

Throughout 1912 and 1913, additional land was granted, and the cemetery nearly doubled its size to almost 1.36 acres. Although it is now closed to new interments, the cemetery is open to the public seven days a week, from 8:00 a.m. until 5:00 p.m., and until 7:00 p.m. on Memorial Day. Hundreds of veterans who have served in several different wars are buried here, many of whom gave their very lives for our freedom.

The Dade Monument, which consists of three coquina pyramid mounds, sits over the top of the remains of 1,468 soldiers who died during the Seminole Wars.

THE INVESTIGATION

Out of all the days to investigate this particular cemetery, I arrived on July 4, 2019. I had the utmost intentions of being as respectful as I could to all the dead buried in this honored ground. Knowing the sacrifices that these soldiers endured, the last thing that I wanted to do was show them any disrespect whatsoever. As I walked through rows and rows of headstones and monuments, I was overwhelmed with how many were interred there, and this was just one of the many cemeteries across the United States where our soldiers were buried. I spent the next few hours investigating the grounds, looking for any evidence of spirits that may still linger there. After several hours with no findings at all, I finally decided to wrap things up. Maybe these soldiers were finally at rest and the cemetery wasn't haunted at all. On the other hand, it may have just been a quiet day for ghost hunting. Regardless, I was honored to be able to spend Independence Day in such a revered location among those who were responsible for protecting the very freedom that we celebrate on that special day.

The cemetery is located on the grounds of the St. Francis Barracks, which is the state headquarters of the Florida National Guard.

THE ARCHITECT'S GHOST:

The Casablanca Inn Investigation

The Casablanca Inn is home to some of the most famous ghost stories in St. Augustine.

A DEVASTATING FIRE

On April 2, 1914, a great fire destroyed every structure north of the Plaza, all the way from St. George Street to the bay. The fire began in the early morning just before daybreak, in the kitchen boiler room of the Florida House over on Treasury Street. A patrolman named S. A. McCormick was walking his beat when he noticed flames erupting from a second-floor window of the Florida House.

The building was soon engulfed in flames before help could arrive. Over the next few hours, six hotels, the opera house, the courthouse, and many other homes and buildings were destroyed. Although the fire destroyed most of the city, there was only one fatality, although numerous others were seriously injured. Alice Smith of Nova Scotia, who was a resident at the Florida house, leapt from the third floor of the building as the fire erupted. She broke her back and was taken to the hospital, where she later died from her injuries.

Later that same year, the building that now houses the Casablanca Inn was constructed over the ashes of the previous building that had existed there and succumbed to the fire. This new structure was designed as an apartment building by architect and civil engineer Goold Butler, who named the place the Matanzas Apartments. Butler not only was the proprietor but lived in the building along with his wife, Hattie. He died a few decades later, in the 1940s, leaving Hattie to live alone as a widow. Interestingly enough, he is also one of the ghosts that has been said to haunt the place.

MR BUTLER'S GHOST

Guests staying in room 11 have encountered his ghost on numerous occasions. One night a few years back, a mother and her three-year-old son were staying in that room. The boy woke up in the middle of the night to a man standing right beside his bed. The child was extremely frightened. The man grabbed his hand and said, "Do not be afraid; my name is Mr. Butler, and I live here." The next morning, the child told his mother what had happened the night before. It wasn't until after they had reported the incident to the staff that they discovered Mr. Butler was the original architect of the house.

MRS. BRADSHAW

One of the most famous ghost stories told about the inn concerns the spirit of a lady named Mrs. Bradshaw. Supposedly in the 1920s, during Prohibition, Mrs. Bradshaw was one of the original owners of the building, and she ran an illegal liquor-smuggling operation there. Rumrunners delivering rum from Cuba would sneak into the bay with their ships. Mrs. Bradshaw would always be waiting on the upstairs porch to watch her cargo arrive. When government officials were nearby, she would wave her lantern back and forth to warn the ships carrying the illegal liquor of their presence, letting them know that it wasn't safe to come ashore. After a few years in this business, she fell in love with one of the young bootleggers, and they soon developed a passionate romance. He later left for Cuba on a liquor run and never returned. The ghost of Mrs. Bradshaw is said to haunt the inn, constantly roaming the halls and the rooms looking for her lost lover. Also, her ghost is known to appear on the upstairs porch, still swinging her lantern back and forth.

Although this makes for a rather interesting tale, there is no evidence that a Mrs. Bradshaw ever lived at this address. I have spent countless hours compiling an entire timeline of the property, which includes a listing of every resident who ever lived at this location, including every single apartment tenant throughout the years. Although there were many people living there during the Prohibition Era, there is no Mr. or Mrs. Bradshaw ever listed as living at this address. Also, in the story she is said to be the owner of the home, yet Mr. Butler, the original owner, and his family owned the building until the 1940s, which was long after Prohibition ended. In addition, there is no evidence to support the idea that there ever was an illegal liquor-smuggling operation at this location.

Throughout the late 1940s and all the way until the early 1990s, the building continued to be used as an apartment building, changing its name several times over the years. It was once the St. John's Apartments, Hawn Apartments, and Brock Apartments. In 1995, after extensive renovations, it reopened as the Casablanca Inn.

Along with the ghost of Mr. Butler, the inn is supposedly home to the ghost of Mrs. Bradshaw as well.

When I initially began conducting investigations in St. Augustine, I knew that the Casablanca Inn was a place that I had to investigate. Ever since I first laid eyes on the place, something seemed to draw me to it. There was a very ominous aura that appeared to surround the structure, and I could never walk past it without a shudder. I could never put my finger on it, but there was definitely something strange about the building that I couldn't quite place.

THE INVESTIGATION

In early August 2019, I arrived late in the afternoon to begin setup for that night's investigation. After spending the next few hours interviewing the staff about the paranormal activity in the building, as well as setting up all the equipment, I was soon ready to begin the investigation. While I was in room 11 conducting an EVP session, I asked, "Who are you?" An EVP was then caught that said, "It's okay." A little while later during the same session, I said, "Mr. Butler, are you here?" An EVP was then caught of a deep male voice that said "Yes." Considering what others had experienced in this very room over the years, I was convinced that I had made direct contact with the very ghost of Mr. Butler himself.

Aside from a few unexplainable fluctuations in temperature and a few small EMF spikes throughout the building, the majority of the evidence I was able to catch during the investigation came from room 11. Does the ghost of Mr. Butler continue to haunt this old building that he designed? It would seem so, and for some reason he seems to like room 11. Also, who is the ghost lady seen roaming the balcony late at night, waving her lantern back and forth? We know now that there never was a Mrs. Bradshaw here. Could this maybe be someone tied to the previous structure who used to live here before it burned down in the fire of 1914? Regardless, the Casablanca Inn continues to be known as one of the most haunted hotels in the city, and the man who originally designed the building still haunts the place. The inn even gained national recognition a few years back for hauntings when the Discovery Channel named it one of the "Ten Most Haunted Hotels in America."

THE LADY IN THE WINDOW:

The Prince of Wales Restaurant Investigation

The hauntings at the Prince of Wales Restaurant are so bad that the previous owner refused to even mention the word "ghost."

At the corner of Cuna and Spanish Streets sits the Prince of Wales Restaurant. According to records, this one-and-one-half-story carpenter Gothic home was built sometime between the years 1865 and 1884. The area was originally developed in the late seventeenth century as a work camp during the construction of the Castillo de San Marcos, and it was later used as a neighborhood after the fort was completed in 1695. All the structures that used to exist here were destroyed in the 1702 siege of the city. The buildings that were north of Cuna Street were destroyed by the Spanish in order to establish a clear field of fire from the fort, and those that were south of the street were demolished by the invading South Carolinians.

The earliest listed occupant of the home was J. C. Ximenies, a grocer. The Ximenies family members were descendants of the Minorcans, who had migrated to St. Augustine from New Smyrna, Florida, in 1777. By 1899, the home had become a boardinghouse, with a chambermaid named Maggie Anderson living there along with P. A. Bradley, who was a laundress and widow. Throughout the early 1900s, Marshall Shelley, who was a driver, lived there. The home continued to change hands numerous times over the next few years, and by 1968 it was acquired by Owen Shelton and his wife, Faye. Owen was a custodian at the Orange Street Elementary School, and Faye was a waitress at the nearby St. George Pharmacy. Faye is also known to be the resident ghost of the restaurant.

THE GHOST OF MRS. FAYE

According to local legend, Faye became a widow a few years later, and she was known to be a very hateful woman. She would yell at anyone who walked past her house. She had become the female version of Ebenezer Scrooge, and people in town couldn't stand her. She was also notoriously cheap. Faye lived on the second floor of the home, and she had a long, narrow staircase she had to climb every night to go to bed. After many years of neglect of her house, the stairs on her staircase became rotted.

Faye hired the cheapest carpenter she could find to repair her staircase. After returning home one afternoon from a shift at the pharmacy, Faye found the carpenter sitting on the porch, taking a small break from the Florida heat. Thinking that he was procrastinating in order to receive more pay, she immediately began screaming at him. The man, who had had enough of her nasty attitude over the past few days, grabbed his tools and quit before finishing the job. Later that evening, Faye awoke in the middle of the night and went downstairs to use the restroom. After taking a couple of steps, one of the rotted stairs broke and she tumbled all the way down the staircase. Four days later, the postman was delivering mail to the house when he noticed an awful smell. All around him was the smell of rot and decay. He lifted the mail slot to slide the mail through the door, and the smell became unbearable. He became sick to his stomach and then he called the police, who found Faye's decomposing body with a broken neck on the other side of the door.

Even though this makes for a great story, it is simply untrue. It is true that Faye along with her husband, Owen, lived in the home, yet Faye died before Owen, proving that she never was an old widow living in the home. In addition,

Faye died on April 20, 1983, of heart disease at Flagler Hospital at the age of seventy-two. She never died in the house, and she didn't die from a broken neck. In addition, there is no evidence to suggest that she was ever this miserly woman that everyone played her out to be.

Although we have disproved the Faye story, the restaurant is haunted by multiple spirits. Many people on ghost tours have seen the apparition of an old woman looking out of the top windows of the home at them, believed to be the ghost of "Mrs. Faye," only to disappear a few moments later. Maybe Faye's spirit haunts this house, or perhaps it's the ghost of one of the many widows who died in the home over the years. Regardless, there is no shortage of paranormal activity here.

FRIGHTENED BY GHOSTS

In 2004, Tony Woodward and his wife, Sharon, bought the house and opened the Prince of Wales Restaurant. The two of them lived in a small, cramped apartment on the second floor of the home and ran their restaurant out of the first floor. Soon after moving into the place, they began to experience hauntings. According to Trish Nease, the restaurant's current manager, who has worked there for the past eleven years, "the Woodwards were extremely frightened by the ghosts here." They wouldn't even talk about the hauntings there or allow anyone to mention them. Every time a ghost tour would stop by and begin talking about the building, Tony would run them off. For the longest time, Trish couldn't understand why he wouldn't embrace it, since it would draw a lot of bar business to the restaurant. One afternoon when Trish asked him about it, Tony said, "Come outside with me." As he and Trish walked outside and away from the restaurant, he said "Trish, I won't allow anyone to talk about the ghosts here because I don't want to wake them." According to Trish, he was extremely frightened but wouldn't talk about what he had encountered there. Soon afterward, the Woodwards sold the building to the current owner, Jake Firth, who continues to operate the restaurant.

Even Trish herself is frightened of the building. She has witnessed doors slam by themselves, and glasses have mysteriously shattered while still sitting on the shelf. She is so frightened that she refuses to close up by herself or even be in the building alone. Even if they are finished before her, she always makes one kitchen employee stay with her until she walks out the door for the night. She said that she can't get out of there quick enough. According to her, it's almost like she can't breathe, and she feels a heavy pressure on her chest. Jokingly, she said, "Maybe it's the ghost of an English woman pissed off that there's an Irish woman running an English pub." Prior to managing the Prince of Wales Restaurant, Trish used to own Ann O'Malley's, which is an Irish pub in town that was named after her mother.

Aside from having the best fish 'n' chips in town, the restaurant has very active ghosts that haunt the place.

THE VISION

When I asked Trish if she had experienced any other paranormal encounters before working there, she recalled a chilling story from her childhood. Trish's sister has always been sensitive to the paranormal. As a little girl in Rotterdam, Netherlands, her sister would wake Trish up in the middle of the night, asking to sleep in bed with her. She would then tell her that she couldn't sleep because there were people in her room. Late one night, she woke Trish up and said that she couldn't sleep because her room was filled with people holding flowers. "No, you must be dreaming," replied Trish. "No, they are really there," her sister added. Trish gave in and let her sister sleep with her that evening. That same night, a boat that was full of children had wrecked nearby. They died holding flowers. The next day after hearing about the shipwreck, Trish asked her sister about it. Her sister then replied, "Those were the people I was telling you about. They were the ones that were in my room last night."

Ever since hearing about the hauntings at the Prince of Wales Restaurant in my good friend James Caskey's book *St. Augustine Ghosts: Hauntings in the Ancient City*, I have had a strong desire to investigate the place. Trish informed me that they would be renovating the restaurant throughout late August and September 2019, and she suggested that we come out and investigate before the renovations commenced. For this case, I teamed up with my colleague and good friend Lauri Carter, who is the founder and lead investigator for the Village Paranormal, based out of Pinehurst, North Carolina. Lauri and I had worked together on numerous cases over the years, most notably the Old South Pittsburg Hospital investigation in Tennessee.

THE INVESTIGATION

As soon as we arrived that evening, we immediately began our initial base readings of temperature and EMF (electromagnetic fields). We noticed a couple of high EMF spikes near an electrical panel box, but nothing out of the ordinary. As soon as the investigation was underway, however, the activity in the building really began to pick up. Oddly enough, the majority of our evidence was captured in the downstairs bathroom. While in there conducting an EVP session, Lauri said, "Show us where you were hurt." Right afterward, a spirit response was captured on one of our audio recorders that replied, "Death." Was this entity saying that they had died there in the building?

A few minutes later, I asked, "Were you a soldier here before this building was built, working on the fort? Or maybe a carpenter or a brick mason?" An EVP was then caught that replied with "Yes." Maybe whoever was haunting this building predated the current structure that exists there. A few minutes after that, we caught the most chilling piece of evidence of the night. Lauri asked, "Can you give us a name?" An EVP was then caught that responded with a voice that growled, "Get back!" As soon as I heard this voice on the playback, the hair on my arms stood on end, and a cold shiver ran down my spine.

A little while later, while we were in the main dining room investigating, we caught another telling piece of evidence. Lauri had said, "So, Faye, did you fall down the stairs and die, or did you die in the hospital?" An EVP was then captured on audio recording that replied, "Died in the hospital." Was perhaps the ghost of Faye haunting her old home even though she didn't die there? Or maybe this was a completely different spirit altogether informing us of where Faye had died? Regardless, it was amazing that we had an EVP response that tied directly to events related to the old building.

Aside from a few uneasy feelings and a few more EVP responses, we didn't capture much else that night, but what we had managed to get during the investigation was awesome. I can't thank Trish and Jake enough for allowing us to investigate this beautiful old house. Should you ever find yourself in St. Augustine, be sure to pop in to the Prince of Wales Restaurant for a plate of fish and chips and a bowl of mushy peas. Upon entering, you will most likely be greeted by Albert, Trish's lovable golden doodle. He brings a lot of character to the place and is one of the friendliest dogs that I have ever had the pleasure of meeting.

CHAPTER 16

THE CEMETERY THAT TIME FORGOT:

The San Sebastian Cemetery Investigation

The Pinehurst and San Sebastian Cemeteries are believed to be the oldest segregated African American cemeteries in Florida.

Only a few miles away from St. Augustine's historic district, in a quieter residential part of town, sits the old San Sebastian Cemetery. It dates back to the late 1800s, when it was first established as an African American cemetery. In 1890, St. Luke's AME Zion Church was built on Pearl Street. In that same year the church began doing burials across the street in what is now the San Sebastian Cemetery. Although the church began putting their dead there in 1890, the oldest burial dates back to 1879, to a man named Warren McKinley. McKinley was born an enslaved person in 1804 and died in 1879. The church continued to use this as an African American burial ground until 2010.

Among those buried in San Sebastian Cemetery is Scipio Miller, who was a Civil War soldier. Sadly, he has no birth date or death date listed, but records show that he was a private in the 33rd US Colored Infantry. He is one of three Union army soldiers who are buried here. The cemetery is also home to African American veterans from the Civil War all the way up to the Korean War. Although the cemetery dates as far back as at least 1879, the first deed of ownership wasn't until 1906, when it was deeded to the San Sebastian Cemetery Association. By 1955, the deeds were transferred to the Pinehurst Cemetery Association. By October 2010, the cemetery was finally closed to new burials.

Among war heroes and the many others buried here, the San Sebastian Cemetery also contains the graves of several enslaved people.

UNMARKED GRAVES

Unfortunately, over the years the San Sebastian Cemetery has fallen into horrible disrepair. Many plots are overgrown, family crypts have collapsed, and there are numerous broken headstones and unmarked graves scattered throughout the property. On Memorial Day 2013, a Florida National Guardsman, Lt. Col. Teresa Frank, and her family were looking for something special to do to honor our soldiers. They decided to begin a cleanup project at San Sebastian Cemetery. Ever since that day, Frank and her family have led the Air Guard cleanup project, and they have worked with various other groups and organizations to repair the dilapidated cemetery. Frank, a member of the 125th Fighter Wing in Jacksonville, said her involvement really began as a way to "remember the real reason" for Memorial Day. Even though the cemetery is still in bad condition, these efforts have definitely helped restore this historic place. Since they began the project, they have uncovered the graves of forty-eight African American veterans, two of which date back to the Civil War.

THE INVESTIGATION

With so much rich history, I was excited to be able to investigate the San Sebastian Cemetery. As I pulled up in front of the old St. Luke's AME Zion Church, I could see part of the cemetery just across the street. Looking from the old iron gates, I couldn't believe that the place was in such bad shape. There were tree roots pushing up tombstones, and entire vaults were caving in. There were very few markers, and the ones I could see were either broken or covered in brush. As I walked through the rows of headstones, I was overcome with a sense of sadness. I couldn't believe that the final resting place for these people had been neglected for so long.

After collecting my thoughts, I began taking photographs of the entire cemetery and its historical markers. Next, I turned on my temperature and EMF meters and started setting up motion sensors. Finally, after everything was set up, I began conducting EVP sessions throughout various areas of the cemetery. After hours of this, I wasn't able to capture even one unexplainable anomaly on any of my equipment. Although that sense of sadness never went away, the cemetery seemed very desolate and quiet throughout the investigation. Perhaps the spirits here were quiet this time and weren't in the mood to communicate, or maybe the cemetery itself isn't actually haunted. Only time will tell, but I personally hope that it isn't haunted, which would mean that all the dead that are buried here have finally moved on to a better place.

If you would like to get involved in the cemetery cleanup project, please contact Lt. Col. Teresa Frank at teresa.frank.1@ang.af.mil. At the time of this writing, there are still approximately seventy graves that have yet to be identified, and many of those are still hidden beneath the soil. It's hoped that with these efforts, this cemetery can be restored to its original state, and all the grave markers can someday be discovered.

Many of the graves and headstones in the cemetery are in bad condition; however, an ongoing renovation project has been working to restore this beautiful burial ground.

CHAPTER 17

PALACE OF THE ODD:

The Ripley's Believe It or Not! Museum Investigation

The building that houses Ripley's was originally a luxurious hotel.

Ever since I was a young child, I have always been fascinated with Robert Ripley and his enormous collection of oddities. He spent his entire life searching the world over for his unique treasures, and there is not another collection like it on Earth. The building located on San Marco Avenue that now houses the Ripley's Believe It or Not! Museum was the very first of many museums around the United States that contained Robert Ripley's private collection. Before the place became the home of Ripley's, it was originally built in 1887 for William G. Warden. Warden was a partner in the Standard Oil Company, along with Henry Flagler and John D. Rockefeller, and he had this immense structure built as a summer retreat for his family, which he named "Castle Warden." Warden played a vital role in the development of St. Augustine, since he was the founder of the city's Gas and Electric Light Company, and he also constructed a school in town called Warden Academy.

Due to their well-known stature in town, the comings and goings of the Warden family were often well documented in the city's various newspapers. Sadly, only eight years after his vacation home was built, Mr. Warden died, in 1895, after being quite ill of health for some time. Throughout the next few years, his widowed wife and their numerous children continued to vacation there. The castle remained vacant throughout most of the 1930s, and in 1940 it was purchased by Norton Raskin, who converted the home into the Castle Warden Hotel. During that same year, Raskin married Pulitzer Prize-winning author Marjorie Kennan Rawlings, who was famous for her novels *The Yearling* and *Cross Creek* as well as numerous other works. The couple had an apartment on the top floor of the place that overlooked the bay and the ocean beyond. In May 1942, Rawlings wrote to her friend and fellow novelist Ellen Glasgow regarding the hotel: "Norton tells an amusing story of two privates coming in from Sunday dinner, but going out as soon as they had been given the menu. He asked them why, and one of them said, 'We were looking for fried possum, and they didn't have it.'"

A DEADLY FIRE

Almost two years later, on Easter Sunday, April 23, 1944, tragedy struck at the Castle Warden when a fire suddenly broke out on the third and fourth floors of the hotel. The fire began at around 11:00 a.m. in the third-floor room 17, occupied by one of the hotel's guests, Miss Betty Neville Richeson, only about an hour and a half after she had checked in. Miss Richeson was the operator of a women's dress shop in her hometown of Jacksonville, Florida. As reported by the newspaper, "Miss Richeson, according to hotel employees, rang for the bell-boy, Bernard Young, when she discovered the fire, believed to have been started by a dropped cigarette, although the burned-out condition of the room prevented first inspections confirming this."

Young went for a fire extinguisher and noticed flames coming from underneath the door to Miss Richeson's room. At the same time, another employee immediately called the fire department. As flames erupted from the building, screams could be heard from the penthouse apartment just above Miss Richeson's room. That room was occupied by Ruth Pickering, who was a good friend of the hotel owner's wife, Marjorie Kennan Rawlings. When the firemen arrived a few moments later and kicked the doors in, both women were found dead with wet towels wrapped around their heads. Both had died from suffocation and smoke asphyxiation, and it is believed that the towels had been used to prevent the inhalation of the deadly smoke. Although there were signs of intense heat, there were no burns on the bodies of the two victims. Immediately, when Mrs. Rawlings learned the fate of her dear friend, she sped over to the Castle Warden.

MR X

According to the employees at the Ripley's Believe It or Not! Museum, the cause of death that fateful day in 1944 may not have been from asphyxiation but from murder. Not long before the fire had begun, a mysterious man checked into the hotel under the ominous name of "Mr. X." While this may at first seem suspicious, it wasn't uncommon for people to check into the hotel under fictitious names to protect their identities. Some were famous people staying there who didn't want to be identified, yet others were using false names to protect the discovery of their illicit affairs.

As the story is told on the Ripley's ghost tour, this Mr. X was actually meeting Miss Richeson at the hotel for a lover's rendezvous. Not long after checking in, the two got into an argument. As the disagreement escalated, Mr. X grabbed Miss Richeson and slammed her head against the fireplace mantle. He then dragged her by her hair across the hallway of the hotel. Mrs. Pickering, who happened to be passing by at the time, witnessed the entire event. Mr. X murdered both women and then set them up to appear as if they had died from smoke inhalation. He then started the fire that destroyed part of the hotel.

This is quite interesting, but there are a few holes in the story as told on the Ripley's tour, as well as by many other ghost tours in St. Augustine. To begin with, no one knows who this "Mr. X" was, but there is no evidence to suggest that he was affiliated with Miss Richeson. Also, the cause of death listed for both women was asphyxiation by smoke inhalation, and none of the police reports suggested any sign of foul play involved in the incident. As tragic as the event was, it would appear that the two women's deaths were caused by a horrible accident and not the result of a double homicide.

A couple of years later, in 1946, Norton Raskin sold the Castle Warden Hotel to Daniel Crawford Jr. Crawford had been the president of the elegant Hotel Philadelphian, located in his hometown of Philadelphia, Pennsylvania. Not long after moving to the city and acquiring the Castle Warden, he became president of the St. Augustine Business and Professional Men's Association, and he was later elected to the presidency of the Beach Association.

ODDITIES MUSEUM

On December 25, 1950, the Castle Warden reopened its doors as the Ripley's Believe It or Not! Museum. Robert Ripley was a frequent visitor to St. Augustine, and he had said many times that the Castle Warden would be the perfect place to display his unique collection of oddities. On many of his visits to the city, he would arrive in his ship, the Mon Lei, which was a 50-foot red Chinese junk ship, complete with a gold-plated anchor. Its gigantic engine was painted to look like a dragon, with whiskers, eyes, and teeth. Sadly, Ripley was never able to see the museum, since it opened about a year and a half after his death. During his lifetime, Robert Ripley traveled to over two hundred countries in search of his strange artifacts and oddities, and he left quite a legacy with his enormous collection. There are now over one hundred Ripley's attractions in ten countries all over the world, but the one located in St. Augustine was the very first to open its doors to the public.

THE INVESTIGATION

Being such a huge fan of Robert Ripley and his life's work, I was thrilled at the opportunity to investigate one of the museums that housed his artifacts. In addition, this was the museum that had started the vast empire of the Ripley's attractions. As soon as I arrived that evening, I could understand how the place had earned the name Castle Warden. The building's massive edifice loomed before me at the entrance. As soon as I walked through the door, I was surrounded by a bizarre collection of strange artifacts. There were items such as a Tibetan drum fashioned from a real human skull, African torture paintings depicting gruesome forms of punishment, a vampire-killing kit, and even a real shrunken head, just to name a few.

As the investigation got underway, I immediately picked up an EVP as we were walking up the staircase to the second floor. My audio recorder picked up a voice that said, "Push me." Was this entity trying to tell me that they had been pushed, or were they merely asking me to push them for some unknown reason? Just a short while later, as I was in the third-floor atrium area of the building, I managed to capture a second EVP. This time it was of a male voice that whispered, "Get this." What was it that these spirits were trying to tell me?

A little later into the night, I caught one of the best EVPs that I have ever captured, and this one was a complete sentence. While I was on the third floor of Castle Warden in the atrium area, I had asked, "Can you show yourself?" An EVP was then captured that replied, "It has to be in some form that you guys can't see." This was amazing, since the entity was answering us with a direct response, yet it refused to manifest itself in any way that we could actually see. I was excited that we were able to get a direct response from an intelligent spirit

Among the many creepy artifacts in the museum, Ripley's features real death masks, ancient torture devices, and a shrunken head.

that haunts the place. We managed to capture a few more strange anomalies throughout the investigation, but this full-sentence EVP that I caught on my audio recorder was the best evidence that we captured during our investigation of the Castle Warden.

There is no doubt in my mind that the Ripley's Believe It or Not! Museum in St. Augustine, Florida, is haunted. Throughout our investigation we were able to capture evidence of multiple spirits that haunt the place. The ghosts of Betty Richeson and Ruth Pickering could be the ones haunting the building, considering the tragic end they met on Easter Sunday of 1944. In addition, with all the strange artifacts that are housed there, I wouldn't be surprised if some of the hauntings at Ripley's were tied to some of the objects in the building, for it is well known in the paranormal community that spirits can be attached to objects as well as to locations.

If you decide to visit the museum, be sure to keep your eyes peeled; there is no telling what could lurk just around the corner. The best part about the place is that you can visit it multiple times and still not see it all. It seems that every time that I return there, I always find something I didn't see before, since the place is chock-full of oddities around every corner.

LAVENDER AND MR T:
The Kenwood Inn Investigation

The resident ghost at the Kenwood Inn has been given the nickname "Lavender." Photo by Bill Slavin.

The Kenwood Inn, located just around the corner from the St. Francis Barracks, is the oldest continuously operating hotel in the city of St. Augustine. The building itself was built sometime between 1865 and 1885, and it is listed as a boardinghouse as early as 1886. Although its name has changed many times over the years of its existence, it has always been an operating hotel. One of its earliest proprietors was Raymond LaBorde, who operated the LaBorde Hotel. A few decades later, in 1911, the hotel changed its name to the Kenwood, which was run by Mrs. J. L. Morgan.

One of the hotel's most well-known residents stayed there during the 1920s, Mrs. Helene E. Hammond, the secretary of the National Society Conservators of American Women. The society's custodian, Luella Day McConnell, was reported to be "the lady known as Lou," who appeared in the 1907 poem by Robert W. Service, "The Shooting of Dan McGrew." The hotel changed hands numerous times over the years, and by 1940 it became the Kenwood Hotel, run by Andrew Hayden and his wife, Edna.

I PITY THE FOOL

The property changed ownership a few more times throughout the next few decades, and in 1970, Raymond Tritton purchased the place and renamed it Mr. T's Inn. While researching the history on this place, when I first saw the name Mr. T in the city directory, I was beyond thrilled. I grew up in the 1980s, and The A-Team was a huge part of my childhood. Unfortunately, it turned out to be Mr. Tritton and not Laurence Tureaud, who had played B. A. Baracus in the hit television show. Regardless, it was still fun seeing the name. Later, in 1981, the home was purchased by Elsie Hedethiemi, and she renamed it the Kenwood Inn, which it remains to this day. In 2008, the inn was purchased by Pat Dobosz, who continues to own and operate this beautiful historic bed-and-breakfast.

LAVENDER

Ever since Pat purchased the Kenwood Inn, there have been strange reports of paranormal activity occurring throughout the building. One of the most well-known spirits that haunt the place is the ghost of a young female named Lavender. Supposedly, many years ago she was the lover of a very prominent doctor in town. She wanted the doctor to leave his wife so that the two of them could be together, but unfortunately for her, he refused. She then threatened to go public and expose their adulterous relationship, so he murdered her. Sadly, the doctor was never charged with the crime, due to his high standing in the community.

Although this may be one of the most famous stories that have been told about the Kenwood Inn throughout the years, there is a very slim chance that this actually happened. To begin with, every time the story is told, the doctor's name is never mentioned. In addition, Lavender has only a first name, so there is no way to see if these people even existed. Also, looking at the inn's over-150-year history, there never was a record of a doctor living at this address, much less a listing for someone named Lavender. If this story were indeed true, there would be more details surrounding the event. Even though this Lavender story is false, the inn's most haunted room, room number 10, is named the Lavender Room.

A few years ago, they were doing renovations in Lavender's room. The walls had been stripped bare and the room was completely empty. Pat was there late one night, when all of a sudden it began to get really cold in the room. Then, out of the corner of her eye, she saw a figure dressed in white dart right out in front of her and rapidly disappear. It was too quick for her to distinguish whether it was a male or a female spirit, since it moved right past her at a very high speed before it quickly disappeared.

Another spirit known to inhabit the inn is the ghost of the home's original owner, Raymond LaBorde. Pat and the employees at the Kenwood like to say that he checked in, but he never checked out. Many guests have reported finding books that they'd packed in their luggage sitting stacked beneath the bed. The books seemed to move on their own, and they couldn't explain how they got under the bed. It is said that this is the ghost of Raymond, who was looking for a good book to read. At the time I conducted my interview, during the renovations on a few of the rooms, according to Pat, workers had their tools disappear and then reappear in the oddest of locations. They would then say something like, "Get the hell out of here, Raymond." They believe that it is the ghost of Raymond causing them so much trouble and moving things around.

THE CAPTAIN'S WIFE

Aside from the ghost of Lavender and Raymond, another entity known to haunt the Kenwood Inn is the ghost of Mitsy. According to local lore, she is an older woman and the widow of a sea captain. Many years ago, she would come to stay at the hotel and wait for her husband's ship to come in. Although she waited for several years, it never arrived, and she supposedly died of a broken heart. She is said to haunt the inn, still waiting on her husband's ship to return. Unfortunately, just like the Lavender story, there is no record that anyone named Mitsy was ever associated with this location. This story is also very likely untrue. It seems that some version of this same tale is told in numerous cities throughout the world that are near the ocean. Many employees as well as guests, however, have reported smelling the distinct fragrance of gardenia, and this scent has been attributed to the presence of the ghost of Mitsy.

Other paranormal occurrences at the inn include guests describing themselves feeling a very heavy pressure making it difficult to breathe, almost as if someone (or something) was pressing down hard on their chest. Many others have reported uneasy feelings while in the building, including extreme cold spots and chills. Some guests have described things being moved by themselves in the middle of the night. They will wake up the next morning and their belongings will be in the strangest of places. One of the more disturbing incidents, however, involves guests seeing the shadow of someone's feet right outside their door, pacing back and forth. They will immediately open the door, only to find no one there and the hallway completely empty.

THE INVESTIGATION

Every time I travel to St. Augustine on business, I try to set up a new investigation in the city, and in many cases it turns out to be a haunted hotel. On September 15, 2019, I arrived just after 3:00 p.m. to check into the Kenwood Inn and begin setting up for that night's investigation. Although the inn is located within St. Augustine's downtown area, it sits just a few blocks away from the main thoroughfares in the city, in a quiet little area on Marine Street. This was great, because a lot of traffic and numerous tourists walking about can cause quite a bit of noise contamination when conducting EVP sessions.

After setting up all the camera equipment, I began conducting base readings of temperature and EMF (electromagnetic energy) throughout the building. Following my base readings, I wandered room to room, scanning with my thermal-imaging camera and my full-spectrum camera, with the hopes of capturing the image of a ghostly apparition. In addition, I conducted numerous EVP sessions throughout the building in an attempt to pick up a spirit voice on my audio recorder. Unfortunately, after many hours of investigating, I wasn't able to find any paranormal anomalies in the inn.

At around 5:00 a.m., I decided to retire to bed. Although I had wanted to stay in Lavender's Room that evening, it was under construction at the time of my visit. Instead, I was sleeping in room number 2, which was also known to be haunted. Right before I went to sleep, I turned on an audio recorder and placed it on the nightstand beside the bed. About a half an hour after I had fallen asleep, an EVP was picked up on the recorder of a small child's voice. Although I have listened to this EVP many times, it was indistinguishable as to what this spirit was saying, but it was unmistakably the voice of a young child. Less than five minutes later, another EVP was captured, but this time it was the voice of an adult that whispered, "Hey, Ryan," as if it were trying to get my attention. Somehow, I managed to sleep through the entire event. It wasn't until the following day when I was reviewing my evidence that I heard the two voices on my audio recorder.

I found it rather interesting that I didn't manage to capture any paranormal evidence during my investigation until after I fell asleep that night. I don't know if the spirits that haunt the place weren't willing to communicate with me, or if maybe it was just an off night. Regardless, I was still pleased that I was able to walk away with some evidence to confirm that the inn was indeed haunted. As far as accommodations, I highly recommend the Kenwood Inn for a nice, relaxing stay in St. Augustine. They have fourteen rooms, as well as a couple of two-room suites, and a beautiful sundeck and outdoor pool. If you visit the inn, make sure that you bring a few books for Raymond, since I hear he is always looking for a good read.

CHAPTER 19

LEVITATING OBJECTS:
The Agustin Inn Investigation

The ghosts at the Agustin Inn tend to be playful and mischievous.

Located along Cuna Street, just a stone's throw away from the Prince of Wales Restaurant, sits the Agustin Inn. This two-story Colonial Revival building was built between the years 1899 and 1904 and is surrounded by a large masonry wall. Prior to the structure being erected on this lot, the land was used in the late 1600s as a work camp for workers who were building the Castillo de San Marcos. This home was originally built for Bernard Masters, who was a wealthy businessman in the cattle industry. He built many homes along Cuna Street and throughout the entire city. His family members were descendants of the Minorcans, who had arrived in St. Augustine from New Smyrna, Florida, in 1777.

In 1916, carpenter Bert Smith lived in the house. By 1918, it became the home of a dressmaker, Mrs. Blanche Miller, who was the widow of Silas Miller. Throughout the 1920s, barber Joseph Grady lived there with his wife, Lena. In 1930, widow Hattie Collins purchased the home, and she continued to live there until 1964, when she passed away, and her daughter, Lucille Collins, inherited the house. Lucille was the principal at the nearby Crookshank Elementary School. During her years in the home, she leased out rooms to Ruth Cook, who was a waitress at the St. George Pharmacy, as well as to a woman named Edith Flynn. By 1989, the house became vacant. Nine years later, in 1998, it was converted into the Agustin Inn, which it remains today.

MYSTERIOUS SHADOW FIGURES

According to Audra Hull, the inn's general manager, there have been numerous reports of paranormal occurrences in the home. One time, shortly after she began working there, Audra saw on the security camera a strange shadow figure in the upstairs hallway dart past and then suddenly vanish into thin air. When she looked again, there was nothing there but an empty hallway.

One afternoon, Gary, the inn's maintenance man, was changing a lightbulb on the third floor. As he was working, one of the managers was standing by, holding the ladder for him for support. When he took the bulb out and held it in his hand, it started to glow. After a few seconds, the light dimmed out. Both of them were astonished as they witnessed this strange event happen.

One of the more disturbing occurrences known to happen at the Agustin Inn concerns levitating objects. Late one night, two guests were at the coffee station fixing a drink when a strange incident happened. One of them had just filled up a cup and turned around to get some sugar. When they turned back, the coffee cup was floating in midair. Another similar incident happened not long afterward. A housekeeper one morning happened to notice that the coffee station was starting to shake by itself. All of a sudden, every one of the coffee cups flew off the station and levitated in the air for a moment. They then settled themselves gently onto the floor. Even more surprising is the fact that not one of the cups was broken.

Many guests staying in rooms toward the back of the house have complained because they will turn the light off in the room and it will come back on all by itself. They will turn the light back off, and later it will come back on again on its own. Other paranormal encounters have included strange apparitions that keep appearing in photographs. Once, a guest staying in room 13 was taking a photo of his wife while they were in the room. In the photo there appeared to be a strange wispy, white entity standing directly beside his wife.

THE INVESTIGATION

Ever since our ghost tour, Afterlife Tours, opened in St. Augustine in fall of 2018, the Agustin Inn has been sending all their guests to us for their haunted tours. It wasn't until about a year later, however, in September 2019, that I was able to investigate the place. After many hours at the St. Augustine Historical Society conducting research on the property, I was able to compile a very interesting history of the home, but nothing I could find that could be the root of the hauntings there.

I did, however, find an interesting tale about the inn in Dave Lapham's book *Ghosts of St. Augustine*. According to his tale, he claims that an elderly woman used to live in the home and that she happened to be a spiritualist. After her death, her niece was at the old woman's home going through her things and getting everything in order. She found an old Ouija board in the house. Soon afterward, paranormal activity began to occur there. The young girl's parents brought a psychic into the home, who said that it was haunted by an old man with "white hair and a close-cropped, white beard; rather a tall man." The girl's mother then claimed that it was the ghost of Chiles, who was her sister-in-law's ex-boyfriend, who had died a few years before.

The problem with his story is that it never mentions any names except for Chiles, whose last name wasn't listed. The story itself doesn't make much sense, and the fact that no specific names were used means that there is no way to verify if this really happened. There were various elderly widows who lived in the home throughout its history, most notably Hattie Collins, but there is no evidence to suggest that any of them were ever involved in spiritualism or the occult.

One of my main objectives during the investigation was to see if I could find out who the entity or entities were that haunted the inn. After the rest of the staff had left for the evening, I was joined by Aubrey Roberts, one of the inn's concierges, as we headed upstairs to begin for the night. Just a little after 8:00 p.m., we were in room 4, and I noticed that the alarm clock on the nightstand said 5:01 p.m. I had been in the room a half an hour earlier conducting base readings, and the clock was reading 7:30 p.m. Somehow it had set itself backward exactly three hours, and no one had entered the room since I was last there.

A few minutes later, while conducting an EVP session, I asked, "Who are you?" An EVP was then picked up on the audio recorder that responded with "Mack." I was excited to get a name for our first EVP of the night, but I wasn't able to find the name in the history of the place. Perhaps it was the name of one of the workers who were there in the late 1600s, building the Castillo de San Marcos. In the same room I was also able to document several unexplainable EMF spikes on my Mel-Meter, which documents temperature and EMF readings, some registering over 20 milligauss.

Just a little while later, the two of us were in room 9 investigating when the activity in the building really began to pick up. Aubrey was using the FLIR thermal-imaging camera when all of a sudden, a dark figure began pacing back and forth right outside the door. It appeared to be the apparition of a woman in a long dress, and she continued to pace outside the door for approximately four minutes, only to suddenly disappear. During that same time, I felt something lightly touch my right shoulder. It felt like a soft hand gently brushing past me. I immediately turned around, and there was nothing, or no one, behind me.

At the same time that the strange apparition was walking back and forth just outside the door, we were conducting an EVP session in the room. After a few minutes with no responses, I asked, "Who are you?" An EVP was then captured that responded with "Helena." It is a very faint EVP, but it was clearly the voice of an old woman. I am strongly convinced that this was the voice of the same entity that was in the hallway just outside the door. Right after the apparition in the hallway disappeared, both Aubrey and I could hear the distinct sound of someone walking back and forth upstairs above us, yet we were the only two in the main house.

Although a few other odd things happened throughout the investigation, it seemed that all the major paranormal activity that we experienced that night happened early on and in a time span of less than thirty minutes. I was pleased that I had gotten what I had come for, which was to get a name of the entity or entities that were haunting this beautiful home. The questions were as follows: Who were these two people, Mack and Helena? And furthermore, what was it that tied them to the house? I hope that as time goes by, we will have an answer, but until then, the spirits there will continue to roam the halls and have frequent interactions with the world of the living. As for the inn itself, there is a reason that it is listed as one of the top hotels in St. Augustine. Their attention to detail and care for their guests is second to none.

44 Spanish Street Inn features several haunted rooms, all of which are fairly active.

In October 2016, Hurricane Matthew devastated the city of St. Augustine, destroying over a thousand buildings in its wake. Just three weeks before the catastrophic event, Brian Funk and his partner Emery McClune purchased the 44 Spanish Street Inn. Although the current building that houses the inn was built in 1924, a previous structure sat on the lot that dated as far back as 1899, which was built for a fisherman named Antonio Pomar. Over the next few years, it was home to an elderly widow and later a plumber named Paul Masters.

The first resident listed in the building that now sits there was Jerome Lopez, who was also a fisherman. The Lopez family was descended from some of the earliest Spanish residents of St. Augustine. By 1927, the home was used as the office of the Pellicer Plumbing Company and then later the Winningham Awning and Shade Company. Throughout the 1930s and 1940s, it was once again a private residence, with various tenants throughout that time period.

By 1953, the house was spilt up into three separate apartments, but by the late 1960s it had been converted into four apartments. This continued until 1986, when it was once again converted into business use, this time as a real estate office and an attorney's practice. In 1989 and 1990, it was home to Sherry Norma, who specialized in facials, massages, and manicures. After a few other businesses came and went, the home was finally converted into a hotel in 2004, which was named the Azalea Inn Bed and Breakfast. Only a short while later, in 2006, it changed its name to the 44 Spanish Street Inn.

A STRANGE DISCOVERY

Ever since Brian and Emery purchased the place in 2016, there have been various reports from both their staff and guests about hauntings within the home. Much of the activity occurs in the room known as the "Zora Neale's Retreat," but strange events have happened elsewhere in the building as well. Not long after they had purchased the place, they decided to pull up the floor in Zora's room to put in a new shower. When they pulled up the floor, an old coquina well was found underneath the home. Some of the house's beams actually sit on the well itself, which is well over two hundred years old. There is still water in the well, and it has old roots growing right through it. After the shower was put in, the floor was replaced, and the well still sits under the building, directly beneath the bed in that room.

One time, a psychic was visiting the inn, and Emery told her about the old coquina well that was under the house beneath "Zora Neale's Retreat." The psychic took a crystal pendulum that she had hanging from a chain necklace and held it directly over the center of the bed that sits over the old well. Within a few seconds, the pendulum began swinging around rapidly in circles by itself, as if it had been propelled by an unseen force. Other guests staying in this particular room have also reported feeling a strange energy while there.

Anna Guevara, one of the inn's housekeepers, and her coworkers have seen the apparitions of people walking in the hallways while they are cleaning the rooms, particularly on the second floor. They will walk out into the hall to see who it is, and there will be no one there. According to Brian, this is known to happen quite frequently. In addition, things in the inn are known to move about on their own. Brian has an old clock that sits on a table in the front lobby of the building. The clock sits toward the very back of the table. On many occasions, he will come in to find that the clock has been moved toward the front of the table. After he moves it back to its original position, he will later find it moved back to the front of the table. This happens when there are no guests in the building.

Employees have witnessed full-bodied apparitions walking the halls of the old inn.

According to Emery, much of the activity that he has experienced at the inn has happened when no one else is in the building. One afternoon, he heard what sounded like someone typing on a computer, and the strange noise was coming from Brian's office. He knew that Brian had left just a short while before, but he thought that maybe he had returned. He went into his office to look to find that it was completely empty, and no one else was in the building. On many other occasions, Emery has heard voices in the building saying "Hello" to him, even when he is the only one there. Many times, he hears the sound coming from the direction of the lobby. He will walk there and the room will be entirely unoccupied, and the front door will be locked.

THE INVESTIGATION

Not long after I had returned home from a recent business trip to St. Augustine, I received a call from one of the owners of the 44 Spanish Street Inn, Brian Funk. I had stopped by just about a week before to drop off some brochures and information about our ghost tour company, Afterlife Tours. Brian was thrilled to find out that our team did all our own historical research and conducted paranormal investigations throughout Savannah, Georgia; St. Augustine, Florida; and other locations in the United States. He then began to tell me about the paranormal activity that he had experienced during his short time owning the inn. We set up an investigation date for a few months later, and I returned in September 2019 to conduct my research.

As soon as I arrived, I was informed by both Brian and Emery that I would be sleeping in "Zora Neale's Retreat" that night. Honestly, I was a little apprehensive about sleeping with my bed sitting directly over an old well, whether there was a floor between the two or not. After I had finished unpacking, I immediately began to conduct base readings of EMF and temperature, as well as a baseline thermal-imaging scan of the entire building. As soon as I entered "Zora's Retreat," my Mel-Meter began to document an extremely high EMF reading directly above the bed in the room. There was nothing electrical nearby that could have caused this high of a spike, and it stopped a few seconds after the reading was captured. A little while later, as I was conducting a thermal scan of the second-floor hallway, I witnessed a shadow figure come right out of the wall and turn to look at me. It then began walking toward me at a very fast rate, and then, right before it got to me, it suddenly disappeared. I was frozen with shock, since I thought that this entity was either going to knock me down or run right through me, but in an instant it was gone.

Later into the evening, I was in "Zora Neale's Retreat" conducting an EVP session. Within the first five minutes, an EVP was caught on an audio recorder that said, "Hide them." This wasn't in response to any questions whatsoever, so I wasn't really sure what this spirit may have been referring to, but the voice itself sounded downright chilling. Just a few minutes later, I captured my second EVP of the night, and this one appeared to be the same voice as the previous one. This time the EVP said, "Get me outta here." Was this spirit possibly trapped there in some kind of limbo between the living and the dead? Whoever this was, it was most definitely the voice of a male spirit.

Later into the night, I decided to head into the back storage room to investigate. As soon as I entered the room, an overwhelming sense of dread seemed to come over me. I can't quite explain it, but it was as if someone, or something, did not want me there. After later speaking with Emery, I was told that he always experienced similar feelings when entering that particular room. I wasn't able to capture evidence there, but something about that room didn't feel right.

A DISTURBING RESPONSE

In the early hours of the morning, I found myself back in "Zora Neale's Retreat" conducting another EVP session. After a few minutes, I asked, "Who are the spirits people have seen walking down the halls?" An EVP was then caught that responded with "Get out." This response seemed to be an ongoing theme in quite a few of the investigations I have conducted in St. Augustine, since I had picked it up on several EVPs in many locations throughout the city. I was getting the feeling that maybe the spirits there didn't want to be bothered and would rather be left alone.

Less than a half an hour later, I was still in the same room when I asked, "What is your name?" An EVP was then picked up on one of my audio recorders that once again responded with "Get out." No matter what type of question I asked, I would receive no response at all, or just someone telling me to get out. Throughout the rest of the investigation that night, the house remained rather quiet. I was able to capture a few other strange things but nothing as concrete as the apparition in the hallway on my thermal camera or the audio I had picked up in the "Zora Neale's Retreat" room. As I lay in bed later that night trying to fall asleep, I couldn't help but have the feeling that I would be sucked down into the pit of some deep abyss while I slept. With the old coquina well sitting directly beneath me, I felt that my slight paranoia was somewhat valid. And besides, who knew what secrets the well itself might have held?

A FINAL FAREWELL

I am not in the least bit surprised that the 44 Spanish Street Inn is listed as the top bed-and-breakfast in St. Augustine on Trip Advisor. Owners Brian Funk and Emery McClune are two of the most gracious hosts that I have ever had the pleasure of meeting. Their attention to detail and their guests is astonishing. As soon as I arrived for my investigation and stay, I felt completely at home from the moment I walked through the door. Sadly, the next morning I had to depart, but I felt that I received the perfect farewell, since I was able to enjoy a marvelous three-course breakfast in the inn's private courtyard. When you visit the inn, please say hello to Henry, their Wheaton terrier, since he is usually in the lobby hanging out during the day, and he is such a friendly dog. If you should decide that you are brave enough, stay in "Zora Neale's Retreat." Good luck and pleasant dreams!

AFTERWORD

Our paranormal research team, the Savannah Ghost Research Society, continues to conduct investigations in St. Augustine and throughout the United States. If you should be in need of our services, feel free to contact us either by phone at (912) 665-8886, or by email at savannahghostresearchsociety@gmail.com.

We also own and operate a walking ghost tour called Afterlife Tours, which features real paranormal evidence that we have captured during our investigations, as well as fact-based ghost stories that have been verified through our historical and paranormal research. We operate our tours both in St. Augustine, Florida, and in Savannah, Georgia. You can book your tour by visiting our website at www.afterlifetours.net, or by calling us at the office at (912) 398-7820. You can also reach us by email at afterlifetours@yahoo.com.

Thank you so much for purchasing this book and for your support.

Author Ryan Dunn with his two daughters, Jenny (left) and Addison (right), and actor Ernie Hudson, who played Winston Zedmore in the Ghostbusters movies.

VISITOR AND CONTACT INFORMATION FOR HAUNTED LOCATIONS

44 Spanish Street Inn
44 Spanish Street
St. Augustine, FL 32084
(904) 826-0650
www.44spanishstreetinn.com

Agustin Inn
29 Cuna Street
St. Augustine, FL 32084
(904) 823-9559
www.agustininn.com

Antiques and Uniques (currently, as of this writing, vacant)
7 Aviles Street
St. Augustine, FL 32084

Casablanca Inn
24 Avenida Menendez
St. Augustine, FL 32084
(904) 829-0928
www.casablancainn.com

Casa de Sueños
20 Cordova Street
St. Augustine, FL 32084
(904) 824-0887
www.casadesuenos.com

Castillo de San Marcos
1 South Castillo Drive
St. Augustine, FL 32084
(904) 829-6506
www.nps.gov/casa/index.htm

Hours of operation:
Sunday to Saturday, 9 a.m. to 5 p.m.
16 and older, $15.00
Children 15 and younger are free

Huguenot Cemetery
8 South Castillo Drive
St. Augustine, FL 32084

Hours of operation:
The cemetery is open to the public on the third Saturday of every month from 11:00 a.m. to 3:00 p.m.

Kenwood Inn
38 Marine Street
St. Augustine, FL 32084
(904) 824-2116
www.thekenwoodinn.com

The Oldest Wooden Schoolhouse
14 St. George Street
St. Augustine, FL 32084
(904) 824-0192
www.oldestwoodenschoolhouse.com

Hours of operation:
Monday to Thursday, 9:00 a.m. to 6:00 p.m.
Friday and Saturday, 9:00 a.m. to 8:00 p.m.
Adults, $5.00
Children 6 to 12, $4.00
Children 5 and under, free

Old Powder House Inn
38 Cordova Street
St. Augustine, FL 32084
(904) 201-2325
www.oldpowderhouse.com

Potter's Wax Museum
31 Orange Street
St. Augustine, FL 32084
(904) 829-9056
www.potterswaxmuseum.com

Hours of operation:
Sunday to Saturday, 9:00 a.m. to 6:00 p.m.
Adults, $12.77
Children 6 to 12, $7.44
Children under 6, free

Prince of Wales Restaurant
54 Cuna Street
St. Augustine, FL 32084
(904) 810-5725

Ripley's Believe It or Not! Museum
19 San Marco Avenue
St. Augustine, FL 32084
(904) 824-1606
www.ripleys.com/staugustine

Hours of operation:
Sunday to Saturday, 10:00 a.m. to 5:00 p.m.
Adults, $15.99
Seniors, $13.00
Children 5 to 11, $9.99
Children under 5, free

San Sebastian Cemetery
710 Pearl Street
St. Augustine, FL 32084
The San Sebastian Cemetery is closed to the public.

Scarlett O'Hara's Restaurant
70 Hypolita Street
St. Augustine, FL 32084
(904) 824-6535
www.scarlettoharas.net
Hours of operation:
Sunday to Saturday, 11:00 a.m. to 1:00 a.m.

St. Augustine Lighthouse
81 Lighthouse Avenue
St. Augustine, FL 32080
(904) 829-0745
www.staugustinelighthouse.org

Hours of operation:
Sunday to Saturday, 9:00 a.m. to 6:00 p.m.
Adults, $12.95
Seniors and children 12 and younger, $10.95

St. Augustine National Cemetery
104 Marine Street
St. Augustine, FL 32084
(904) 766-5222
Hours of operation:
Sunday to Saturday, 8:00 a.m. to 5:00 p.m.

St. Francis Inn
279 St. George Street
St. Augustine, FL 32084
(904) 824-6068
www.stfrancisinn.com

Tolomato Cemetery
14 Cordova Street
St. Augustine, FL 32084
www.tolomatocemetery.com

Hours of operation:
The cemetery is open to the public on the third Saturday of every month from 11:00 a.m. to 3:00 p.m.

BIBLIOGRAPHY

Arnade, Charles W. The Siege of St. Augustine in 1702. University of Florida Monographs, Social Sciences 3, Summer 1959. Whitefish, MT: Literary Licensing, 2011.

Auerbach, Loyd. *ESP, Hauntings, and Poltergeists: A Parapsychologist's Handbook.* New York: Warner Books, 1986.

Baird, Charles Washington. *History of the Huguenot Emigration to America.* Vol. 1. Charleston, SC: BiblioBazaar, 2010.

Barrett, S. M., and Geronimo. *Geronimo: The True Story of America's Most Ferocious Warrior.* New York: Skyhorse, 2011.

Beeson, Kenneth H., Jr. *Fromajadas and Indigo: The Minorcan Colony in Florida.* Mt. Pleasant, SC: History Press, 2006.

Bradford, Ernle. *Drake: England's Greatest Seafarer.* New York: Open Road Media, 2014.

Caskey, James. St. Augustine's Ghosts: Hauntings in the Holy City. Savannah, GA: Manta Ray Books, 2016.

Clark, James C. *A Concise History of Florida.* Mt. Pleasant, SC: History Press, 2014.

Considine, Bob. *Ripley: The Modern Marco Polo.* Whitefish, MT: Literary Licensing, 2013.

Dunn, Ryan. *Savannah's Afterlife: True Tales of a Paranormal Investigator.* Atglen, PA: Schiffer, 2014.

Dunn, Ryan. *Savannah's Afterlife II: More True Tales of a Paranormal Investigator*. Atglen, PA: Schiffer, 2018.

Estep, Sarah Wilson. *Voices of Eternity*. New York: Fawcett, 1988.

Fairbanks, George. *The Spaniards in Florida: Comprising the Notable Settlement of the Huguenots in 1564, and the History and Antiquities of St. Augustine, Founded 1565*. Whitefish, MT: Kessinger, 2009.

Gannon, Michael V. *The Cross in the Sand: The Early Catholic Church in Florida, 1513–1870*. Gainesville: University of Florida Press, 1983.

Gannon, Michael V. *Rebel Bishop: The Life and Era of Augustin Verot*. Milwaukee, WI: Bruce, 1964.

Griffin, Patricia S. *Mullet on the Beach: The Minorcans of Florida, 1768–1788*. Gainesville: Library Press at University of Florida, 2017.

Guiley, Rosemary Ellen. *The Encyclopedia of Ghosts and Spirits*. New York: Checkmark Books, 2007.

Harter, Walter L. *Osceola's Head and Other Ghost Stories*. Upper Saddle River, NJ: Prentice Hall, 1974.

Harvey, Karen. *St. Augustine's Ghosts*. Gainesville, FL: Seaside, 2018.

Hatch, Thom. *Osceola and the Great Seminole War: A Struggle for Justice and Freedom*. New York: Macmillan, 2012.

Holzer, Hans. *America's Haunted Houses: Public and Private*. Stamford, CT: Longmeadow, 1991.

Kaserman, James F., Sarah Kaserman, and Sarah Jane Kaserman. *Florida Pirates: From the Southern Gulf Coast to the Keys and Beyond*. Mt. Pleasant, SC: History Press, 2011.

Knetsch, Joe. *Florida's Seminole Wars, 1817–1858*. Mt. Pleasant, SC: Arcadia, 2003.

Lapham, Dave. *Ghosts of St. Augustine*. Sarasota, FL: Pineapple, 1997.

Leach, Mike, and Buddy Levy. *Geronimo: Leadership Strategies of an American Warrior*. New York: Gallery Books, 2014.

Lee, K. Ross, and Betsy S. Lee. *Andrew Ranson: St. Augustine's Pirate*. Elkton, FL: K. B. Aren, 2014.

Lyon, Eugene. *The Enterprise of Florida: Pedro Menéndez de Avilés and the Spanish Conquest of 1565–1568*. Gainesville: University Press of Florida, 1983.

MacColl, Letitia. *The Story of Sir Francis Drake*. Buffalo, NY: Creative Media Partners, 2017.

Manucy, Albert. *The Building of the Castillo de San Marcos.* Bronson Tweed, 2014.

Manucy, Albert. *Menéndez: Pedro Menéndez de Avilés, Captain General of the Ocean Sea.* Sarasota, FL: Pineapple1992.

Manucy, Albert. *Sixteenth-Century St. Augustine: The People and Their Homes.* Gainesville: University Press of Florida, 2008.

Missall, John, and Lou Missall. *The Seminole Struggle: A History of America's Longest Indian War.* Sarasota, FL: Pineapple, 2019.

Mitchell, Florence. *A History of Huguenot Cemetery, 1821–1884, St. Augustine, Florida.* St. Augustine, FL: Friends of the Huguenot Cemetery, 1998.

Monaco, C. S. *The Second Seminole War and the Limits of American Aggression.* Baltimore: Johns Hopkins University Press, 2019.

Price, Harry. *Confessions of a Ghost Hunter.* New York: Time-Life, 1993.

Randall, Elizabeth. *Haunted St. Augustine and St. John's County.* Haunted America. Charleston, SC: History Press, 2013.

Rawlings, Marjorie Kinnan. *Cross Creek.* New York: Charles Scribner's Sons, 1942.

Rawlings, Marjorie Kinnan. *The Yearling.* New York: Charles Scribner's Sons, 1938.

Sammons, Sandra. *Henry Flagler, Builder of Florida.* Sarasota, FL: Pineapple, 2010.

Sammons, Sandra. *Ponce de Leon and the Discovery of Florida.* Sarasota, FL: Pineapple, 2013.

Simms, William Gilmore. *The Lily and the Totem, or, The Huguenots in Florida: A Series of Sketches, Picturesque and Historical, of the Colonies of Coligni, in North America, 1562–1570.* Columbia: University of South Carolina Press, 2016.

Slavicek, Louise Chipley. *Juan Ponce de León.* New York: Facts on File, 2003.

Standiford, Les. *Last Train to Paradise: Henry Flagler and the Spectacular Rise and Fall of the Railroad That Crossed an Ocean.* Portland, OR: Broadway Books, 2003.

Sugden, John. *Sir Francis Drake.* London: Pimlico, 2006.

Tebeau, Charles W. *A History of Florida.* Miami, FL: University of Miami Press, 1971.

Thompson, Neal. *A Curious Man: The Strange and Brilliant Life of Robert "Believe It or Not!" Ripley.* New

York: Three Rivers, 2014.

Warren, Ed, and Lorraine Warren, with Gerald Brittle. *The Demonologist.* Englewood Cliffs, NJ: Prentice-Hall, 1980.

Ryan Dunn, along with his wife Kim, owns and operates the Savannah Ghost Research Society, which they founded in 2010. They also own Afterlife Tours, a walking ghost tour that features real paranormal evidence from their team's findings. They have been featured on A&E Biography's My Ghost Story: Caught on Camera, SyFy Channel's Paranormal Witness, CMT's Party Down South, as well as other networks. They also have their own television show entitled Spooky Town with WJCL-ABC News and Fox News 28 here in Savannah. The Dunns live in a haunted house in Savannah's historic district with their two daughters, Jennifer and Addison, along with their son, an English Bulldog named Griswold.